For the
LOVE OF AIMEE

Toni,
Love &
Blessings!
Julie

For the
LOVE OF AIMEE

A MEMOIR

JULIE RIERA MATSUSHIMA

EMERALD
BOOK CO.

Note: This is a work of nonfiction. The details presented are the personal recollection of events to the best of the author's knowledge. Some names and details have been changed to protect the privacy of certain individuals.

Published by Emerald Book Company
Austin, TX
www.emeraldbookcompany.com

Distributed by Emerald Book Company

For ordering information or special discounts for bulk purchases, please contact Emerald Book Company at PO Box 91869, Austin, TX 78709, 512.891.6100 or http://www.juliematsu.com

Design and composition by Greenleaf Book Group LLC and Bumpy Design
Cover design by Greenleaf Book Group LLC
Cover photo by Janna Doucette

Publisher's Cataloging-In-Publication Data
(Prepared by The Donohue Group, Inc.)
Matsushima, Julie Riera.
   For the love of Aimee : a memoir / Julie Riera Matsushima. -- 1st ed.
      p. : col. ill. ; cm.
   Includes bibliographical references.
   ISBN: 978-1-934572-60-3
   1. Cerebral palsied children--Rehabilitation. 2. Cerebral palsied children--Family relationships. 3. Cerebral palsied children--Anecdotes. 4. Grandparent and child--Anecdotes. I. Title.
HV903 .M18 2011
362.1/9836   2010935408

Part of the Tree Neutral® program, which offsets the number of trees consumed in the production and printing of this book by taking proactive steps, such as planting trees in direct proportion to the number of trees used: www.treeneutral.com

TreeNeutral®

Printed in the United States of America on acid-free paper

11 12 13 14 15 10 9 8 7 6 5 4 3 2 1

First Edition

To Chloe and Jeffrey

Joys of My Heart

CONTENTS

ACKNOWLEDGMENTS

Six years have passed in the writing of this book. During that time, there were many starts and stops, often due to circumstances beyond my control. But in the end, I persevered and, finally, accomplished my goal. I would like to acknowledge those who encouraged me from the beginning to tell our story to the world.

I am most grateful to Aimee's parents, Janise and my son, Jason, for their love and trust in me to participate in Aimee's life from the beginning, and for their permission to write this story.

I cannot begin to express the love and gratitude I owe my husband, Mel, for sharing my dreams, at any cost, without a negative thought or word. His tolerance during countless hours of reading one revised manuscript after another stretched his patience beyond what anyone should have to endure, yet he did so with enthusiasm and praise. Thank you for your boundless generosity and for being my light, my crutch, and my safe harbor through it all.

Heartfelt appreciation, beyond words, goes to my daughter Janna Doucette, for immeasurable hours of her time and talent from concept to finish. In addition to a multitude of tasks, she and her husband, Greg, designed an awesome website for me and supplied hours of technical support.

Special thanks to cherished friends: Susan Goldberg and Dave Rich for sharing their expertise to critique my writing and provide me with the encouragement and motivation to remain on course; Father Pat Browne for his prayers, masses, and blessings to keep us safe in our travels; and Doctor Mario Cordero for his willingness to help, professionally or otherwise.

To my family and friends: too many to mention, but you know who you are; thank you for believing in me and for touching Aimee's life in so many special ways. We shall both be forever grateful for your love and support.

To Greenleaf Book Group—especially Matthew Donnelley, Hobbs Allison, Brian Phillips, and Lari Bishop—immense gratitude and heartfelt appreciation for making the book a reality.

THE BEGINNING

CHAPTER 1

IT IS EARLY MORNING ON JANUARY 1, 2001, and it is freezing cold. We've been flying all night, right through the New Year holiday, and are on the final leg of our journey from San Francisco to Chicago, Chicago to Warsaw, and Warsaw to Szczecin, Poland. Our final destination is Mielno, Poland, to Euromed Rehabilitation Center, still about eight hours and a long bus ride away. What in the world am I doing here? I recalled my son's parting words at the airport in San Francisco. "Mom," he said, "be careful. You're responsible for my wife, the baby, and Aimee. Don't let anything happen to my family."

I'm exhausted from having to carry and load our luggage into the belly of this small, old, two-engine airplane. It's snowing and we are rushing to remain dry and get inside. Finally, we're buckled in our seats and I take the opportunity to look around. I notice that none of the thirty passenger seats on this plane are the same. Each one has been cannibalized from different aircraft. But they are, at least, bolted to the floor. Still, I'm frightened.

I look over at Aimee and she smiles in response. Janise, on my opposite side, is five months pregnant, pale, and tired. At this point, I'm concerned about both of them. Soon the plane begins to move and we are speeding down the runway as it rattles and shakes in preparation for takeoff. I put my head back, take a deep breath, grab Aimee's little hand, and squeeze tight. I say a prayer for us. I recall the day she was born and how it has brought us to this moment.

• • •

It is often said that becoming a grandparent is one of the most gratifying experiences in life. And so it was with that splendid feeling of excitement and expectation that I went to sleep the night before my twin granddaughters were born.

I was walking through a quiet park-like garden of large trees, clipped hedges, and flower beds. I was startled when I unexpectedly came upon a large iron birdcage. I felt a strange sense of foreboding as I walked closer to look inside. Perched high on a swing was a gorgeous little bird with colorful plumage and big, alert eyes. I wondered what kind of species this beautiful bird could be, and I watched in amazement as it chirped and sang. Then a very faint "peep" sound met my ears. My eyes followed the sound to the bottom of the cage. Huddled in the corner was an identical, though frail and sickly, little bird. It was so thin and pathetic that I immediately felt a profound sadness. I wanted to do something but felt helpless when I could not open the cage.

I awoke from my dream suddenly, eyes filled with tears and overcome with grief. I was in a state of panic. Head throbbing, I looked at the clock. It was 5:00 a.m. I needed more sleep and finally got out of bed an hour later, still exhausted and unable to shake my feelings of doom and sadness.

In spite of my pounding headache, I remained excited and anxious about becoming a grandmother, and the day had finally arrived! I didn't know it then, but that day was destined to be one of those rare days in a lifetime when you experience the height of happiness and the depth of despair at the same time. At that moment, though, I was angry with myself for scheduling an 8:00 a.m. appointment at my office with a prospective client. Why did I agree to do that? My daughter-in-law, Janise, was scheduled for a C-section at noon, and I had no intention of being late under any circumstances.

• • •

The physician I was scheduled to meet with that morning did not show. His wife arrived instead. She apologized, explaining that he had had an emergency with his disabled daughter. His daughter, she elaborated, was his sole responsibility, having been abandoned by her mother as an infant. She then talked about the hardships and obligations of parenting a twenty-year-old special-needs girl with cerebral palsy. I listened with compassion. After our business concluded, I headed for the hospital.

• • •

It was almost noon when I arrived. Although outwardly cheerful, inside I remained extremely concerned about my daughter-in-law and hoped all would go well. No matter how positive I tried to be, I couldn't seem to shake the gloom that followed me from my dream the night before, and that was heightened by the story from the woman I had just met.

Everyone was at the hospital when I arrived—my husband Mel; my son Jason; his father, my ex-husband, with his wife; Janise's mother, Jackie; and Janise's father with his wife. They all appeared calm. Jason was happy and in good spirits and eager for things to begin. I, on the other hand, continued to feel my excitement give way to apprehension.

• • •

I began to reflect on the events leading up to this day. It had been confirmed early in her pregnancy that Janise was carrying identical twin girls, which required regularly scheduled ultrasounds. All seemed normal and routine up until three weeks ago when Jason and Janise were told that there was a potential problem. One of the twins was now smaller and had a "dark spot" the size of a coin on the top of her skull. It was possibly a small blood clot or cyst, and the doctors said it was nothing that couldn't be handled after the birth. It was not serious enough to take the twins early, they reassured us.

Janise was extremely worried when she heard this news, and she told me about it that evening. Worried too, I immediately went into action. I called our dear family friend, Mario Cordero, a well-known and well-respected obstetrician. Over dinner that evening he expressed his concern but explained that it would be unethical for him to become involved. However, he advised us to seek a second opinion by having a different physician perform an ultrasound. His call to a colleague in Palo Alto secured us an appointment within the week.

We listened intently to the consulting physician's explanation of his findings. He concluded that the dark spot probably was a cyst, or possibly something more serious, but because Janise was only weeks from her due date, he recommended waiting for her C-section as scheduled. I didn't buy it. The twins were almost full term. In my opinion, the risk of potential brain damage seemed greater than the risk of any other early-birth complication. My concerns lingered. Mel and I encouraged Janise to remain calm, but we knew she was deeply troubled by this unexpected turn of events.

Mel, sensing my anxiety, encouraged me to remain positive, and I made every attempt to do so. We were overjoyed at the prospect of having twins in the family. Mel reminded me of the fun we had one evening talking about it with Jason and Janise while discussing names for the babies. I adored the name Chloe from the start. Janise loved the name Amy because she had had a favorite childhood doll with that name. Jason, however, remembered an unpleasant girl from elementary school whom he didn't like, named Amy. He preferred the French spelling— "Aimee." We had many laughs remembering all the nuances associated with names. I was secretly thrilled when they finally announced that each of the girls would be given a middle name honoring their grandmothers. They decided on Chloe Ellen, for Jackie's middle name, and Aimee Marie, for my middle name.

• • •

Chloe Ellen and Aimee Marie were scheduled to come into the world together on Thursday, August 21, 1997, at 12:20 p.m. Eagerly awaiting their arrival, the grandparents held hands outside the delivery room. Stretching to see and listening for any significant sound that would indicate things were happening, we suddenly heard a shriek of joy and a baby's wail. Within moments, the nurse flew into the hall, baby in arms, and exclaimed, "It's a beautiful girl!" as she carried Chloe into the next room.

My first glimpse of Chloe, as she whizzed by, was that of a chubby baby with lots of brown hair. Her mouth was wide open, exclaiming to the world that she had arrived. Oh my God, I thought, she looks just like Jackie. How amazing that a child at the moment of birth can look so much like someone in the family! We hugged, cried, and congratulated each other as new grandparents.

Our joy turned to concern when, within moments, another nurse ran from the delivery room carrying Aimee. The baby was silent, wrapped tightly, and held against her chest. The nurse disappeared into the neonatal ICU. Jason, dressed in scrubs, ran behind her. We didn't get a good look at her but were somewhat relieved that Aimee appeared okay at first glance and that both girls were here and the delivery had been uneventful.

We waited and soon a nurse brought Chloe out for us to meet. She was adorable. We fell in love at first sight. A few moments later Jason returned from the ICU, visibly happy, but concerned that Aimee was placed in intensive care for examination and testing. He left us to return to Janise. After a reasonable period of well-deserved privacy, we joined them in a flurry of hugs, kisses, and good wishes.

We were all so happy at that moment.

The twins were alive and well and Janise was returned to her room. Relieved, we went to the cafeteria for something to eat. On the way, I stopped to call my mother and daughter to inform them that the delivery went well but that we were waiting for news about Aimee. I agreed to call them again when I knew the results of her tests.

The hours slowly ticked away. It was 4:00 p.m. and we'd still received no word. Janise was resting with Chloe in her room. Jason was making calls to friends and family. Surely, we would hear something soon.

I tried but could not shake the memory of my dream from the night before. It conjured up all sorts of distressing thoughts. A chill came over me when I recalled the two little birds. Had it been a bad omen? Finally, when I couldn't stand it any longer, I went to the intensive care unit to see if it was possible to visit Aimee. I was granted permission, but only for a few moments.

I scrubbed and robed as instructed, and then quietly tiptoed inside to see her for the first time. Frightened and worried, I leaned over her little bed and saw that she was connected to various tubes and monitors. My heart broke at the sight of her. Overwhelmed, my tears of joy and happiness mingled with tears of fear and concern as the nurse walked over and placed Aimee in my arms. While not abnormally small, she appeared frail. Yet she was absolutely beautiful. Fingers and toes all present, she was perfectly formed. I stroked her head and became perplexed as I felt and saw the ridges on her skull. I wondered what they were. I lingered a moment longer and then was asked to leave. Seeing her and holding her, if only for a few minutes, brought me great relief and happiness.

The hours passed and we'd still received no news about Aimee. By 6:00 p.m. my husband and I were greatly concerned. Our sense of relief diminished. Our friend Mario joined us at the hospital after finishing his office hours. Aware of the situation, he also expressed worry. He checked in on Aimee and thought she looked good. We were encouraged by that ray of hope that our fears were unfounded; nevertheless, Mario was perplexed that there was still no report. He left shortly thereafter, assuring me that he would check in soon. We were still playing the waiting game when Mario called at 6:30 p.m. to ask if we knew anything yet. We didn't. I remember his words well. "Matsu," he said, "it doesn't look good. They're not saying anything and it has been too many hours. The MRI would have been read immediately." He said he would check back in another hour.

. . .

Jason and Janise were anxious to hear from someone—anyone. They had asked what was happening throughout the afternoon, but the staff were vague and evasive. That worried them more. I had worked in a hospital for years and with physicians on a daily basis at my medical billing company. I understood how they operated. Suspicious, none of us wanted to leave. We were relieved when the doctor finally met with us shortly after 7:00 p.m.

The doctor, a pediatric neurologist, introduced himself and asked everyone except Jason to leave the room and wait at the end of the hall. He wanted to talk privately with the parents first and assured us he would speak with us next. Jason and Janise held hands and feigned courage as their faces turned paste white with fear.

Outside the room, we could hear the doctor's voice but not what he said. We waited in silence, knowing it must be serious. Just how serious became apparent when we heard Janise's scream. We heard Jason attempt to comfort her as they tried to comprehend what the doctor was saying.

I was grief-stricken and trembling in fear when Jason and the doctor stepped out of the room together. Jason's face said it all. I knew it was bad. The test results were devastating. The doctor began to explain the magnitude of Aimee's condition. It was far, far beyond anything we could have imagined.

We held hands as he spoke, drawing strength from one another. I was shaking so much I thought my knees would buckle. A shadow had suddenly darkened this wonderful day, as if a cloud had blocked out the sun forever. It seemed absolutely impossible that the beautiful baby I held only hours before was so damaged. I looked into the eyes of the others and saw the reflection of my own despair.

Aimee had massive brain damage, confirmed by the MRI, from a lack of oxygen some time near the end of the pregnancy. She was diagnosed with microcephaly and cerebral palsy. The neurologist would not speculate on the extent of the damage but conceded that it was severe. His words left us dazed.

What did it mean? We asked many questions, but her team of doctors said they didn't know exactly how or why it had happened.

More bad news followed. Aimee's other physicians said that she probably would not live for more than a few days—perhaps weeks, months at best. The prognosis was so grim, they explained, that in all likelihood she would have a massive seizure within days that would take her life.

I was heartbroken for my son, Janise, and baby Chloe. What was in store for them? How would they cope? What were they going to do? What could I do to help? They were newlyweds, just starting out. This would surely change their lives forever.

Aimee remained in the neonatal ICU, and Jason slept at the hospital with Janise and Chloe in one room. They needed to be together and desperately needed each other's love and support. We honored their time alone. On the way home I called Mario and repeated what we were told.

He was stunned but encouraged us to remain hopeful until we knew all the facts. He assured me that he would help us by finding out whatever he could. I arrived home exhausted and drained. In tears, I telephoned my mother and then my daughter to share the information as I had promised. I could not talk to anyone else. I just wanted to crawl into bed with my sorrow.

But I couldn't sleep. I simply could not believe the turn of events. I thought about the excitement, planning, and expectations we had shared. Today everything had changed and taken on a different meaning. It was a horrible night. I thought about the past and was preoccupied with the future. Inconsolable and fearful, I wept for the babies and their parents.

As a mother, I felt despair for my son. He had recently graduated from college and started his career, working hard and saving to purchase a condominium. Happy and looking toward the future, he had just been hit with a devastating blow.

• • •

Jason and Janise would be celebrating their first anniversary in just two weeks. A strange incident that happened months before their wedding suddenly came to mind. Janise's father, John, and his wife, Liz, consulted on occasion with a psychic friend. During one consultation, the woman asked them about their daughter's wedding. She told them that "two very old spirits are waiting to come, and your daughter will soon be pregnant with twin girls." Her comments were amusing and humorous when Janise shared them with us. We laughed and joked about it for weeks—that is, until Janise became pregnant with twins three months after the wedding. Remembering the prediction, we were awestruck when she announced that she was having identical twin girls.

Janise had been an employee at my medical billing company when she moved to San Jose, and she continued to work throughout her pregnancy. I needed medical billers and she needed a job; it was a win-win for us both. At that time, my company had thirty employees. Another woman on the staff, Nora, was also pregnant with identical twin girls. The fact that two co-workers were having identical twin girls delighted the entire staff. The fact that my nephew and his wife were also expecting twin girls in August made it all seem like a strange coincidence.

Four months into her pregnancy, Nora was told her twins had Down syndrome. Her grief overshadowed the workplace for days. Two weeks later, repeat testing confirmed that the first test was a false negative. We all breathed a deep sigh of relief, and things returned to normal. Eight dozen pink balloons were delivered to the office to wish the expectant mothers well as they left for maternity leave.

I remembered how very concerned I had been over someone else's problem—yet relieved that it wasn't happening to our family. I felt guilty for feeling that way now; the situation was reversed and I felt that life was unfair. My momentary joy was shattered by the sadness of Aimee's condition.

Everything appears magnified during the night. That night was no exception. Every fear came to the surface and threw me into a panic as I tried to sort it all out in my mind.

Surprisingly, on Friday morning, I awoke with a new resolve. Falling apart was not going to help anyone. I had to remain strong, focused, and supportive. Jason and Janise needed our help. They were not alone—they had family that would help in whatever way necessary. They could count on Mel and me. I was determined to learn as much as I could about Aimee's condition. Knowledge would provide direction and open the door to assistance and understanding.

• • •

Returning to the hospital in the morning, I first visited Janise and Chloe. Jason was there also, but he was so weary I could hardly look at him. All he said to me was, "Why? Why us?" I knew he felt overwhelmed, heartsick, and exhausted from moving between the hospital units to spend equal time with both babies. Janise was in a fog, heavily medicated. They were clearly devastated, but I was impressed and deeply moved by the faith and strength they exhibited during this darkest time. Janise's mother remained in the room to help with Chloe and deal with the unending phone calls.

Chloe was thriving and doing well. To confirm that Aimee's condition was solely due to an incident and not any genetic syndrome, the same tests were performed on Chloe. All test results were negative. Examination of the placenta confirmed that, in fact, Aimee and Chloe were identical, mirror-image twins, naturally at the highest risk during pregnancy.

Mario returned to the hospital that afternoon. As a favor to us, he made arrangements with the radiologist, whom he knew, to show us Aimee's MRI. Because Mel had Friday afternoon off, he joined us. We were horrified by what we saw.

The radiologist provided us with a visual and verbal interpretation of the film. The deficiency of brain tissue was extensive. We stood in silence and disbelief as we looked at the MRI on the wall that confirmed the diagnosis of microcephaly. What appeared to have been the upper half of Aimee's brain was destroyed by lack of oxygen. The MRI outlined the skull, but the center appeared to be a dark, black cavity without substance. With the exception of some fibers, it was completely gone. "If the brain is gone," I asked, "what is in its place?" The radiologist responded, "cerebral spinal fluid." I felt nauseated and numb. Mel held my arm to stabilize me. I was in total shock.

The term "microcephaly" was now defined and the explanation for the ridges on Aimee's skull became clear. Because her head had been squeezed, the normal "soft spot" on a baby's head did not exist for her. Instead, her skull had been pushed together as brain mass diminished, and it overlapped, forming ridges.

• • •

Aimee remained in the neonatal ICU and that is where I spent as much time as I could. Aimee's doctor explained that she was at risk of a massive seizure, which could kill her immediately. He suspected that she would not make it through the weekend; if she lived, it would most likely not be for long. He told me that, occasionally, children can live with only a brain stem, but they would never walk, talk, see, or hear. Aimee, he said, would be a quadriplegic, existing in a vegetative state all of her life. The prognosis was appalling and unimaginable. It seemed impossible that this was happening to *our* family. I sobbed uncontrollably off and on for days.

I didn't want Aimee to be alone in the ICU. I held her, talked to her, and fed her. Something magical happened between us. We bonded and I fell in love. She amazed me every time she moved her little head. She seemed so alert, so much more aware than her prognosis seemed to imply. I observed that she appeared to respond to sounds and startled when the nurse dropped a metal container on the floor. How could she be deaf? I wondered.

I was certain she was not deaf. Beyond that, I simply could not, and would not, allow myself to believe everything the doctors said. They had to be wrong some of the time. Haven't doctors been wrong before? I didn't know how I would accomplish it, but I made up my mind then and there to do all I could to help Aimee achieve her maximum potential in life—whatever that could or would be—to help her be the best she could be.

For starters, I would pray. And pray I did: "Dear God, please be merciful and give her something, anything that would make her life easier. Please give her sight, a voice, or the ability to hear. Please don't take everything away." I was not the only one praying. There were hundreds, if not thousands, of prayers for Aimee.

In my heart, I believe that it was the power of so many prayers from so many people that granted Aimee the gifts she has received and the achievements she has accomplished in her short lifetime.

• • •

When Jason visited the ICU later that afternoon, we overheard a staff conversation in another room regarding Aimee and her prognosis. Aimee's physician was discussing the limited options available for her, if she lived, and said it was in the best interest of the family to institutionalize her. There was no advantage, they concluded, in keeping her in the hospital, and they were surprised that she was still alive. Curious, Jason approached the doctor involved and asked him why the conversation was taking place without him. That doctor told him there was nothing else they could do for Aimee. If he and Janise wished, the hospital staff would make arrangements to institutionalize Aimee at an appropriate facility so they wouldn't have to take her home.

Jason hit the ceiling. He demanded that they take her home, with her twin sister, where she belonged and where her family would love and care for her. How many times could my heart break in a day? I listened to Jason's comments with a feeling of pride and love. He valued life; I had taught him well. His love, responsibility, and respect for Aimee's life were apparent. He wasn't going to give up on her, no matter what the doctors had to say. I couldn't have agreed with him more.

Before leaving the hospital that day, I visited Janise again. She was doing better, but, heavily medicated, she thought she was dreaming until her mother gently confirmed the reality. She asked me about Aimee. I gladly shared my observations with her. I told her that Aimee was beautiful, thriving, and appeared responsive.

Unfortunately, Janise was not allowed to leave her unit to visit Aimee. Aimee also could not be moved from the ICU. We didn't understand the reason behind this rule and hoped that they could be together soon. Meanwhile, Chloe continued to do well and was ready to go home.

• • •

By Saturday, Aimee had surprised the staff with her stamina; she was eating well and remained stable. The best news of all was the absence of the predicted seizures. Other than Jason and me, those who came to see Aimee were timid and afraid to hold her for any period of time. It was obvious to me that her beautiful but frail body deeply saddened everyone who visited her. After a brief stay they would leave without a word, as if attending a memorial service.

Jason busied himself with making plans and preparations for the homecoming. He returned to the hospital late in the day, enthusiastic and ready to take his family home. He had installed the matching baby seats in the car and was ready to transport the girls.

Janise was still attempting to deal with the realities of the situation. Rightfully depressed, she continued to have crying fits of sorrow but was coping the best she could. Eager to see Aimee but also frightened, she didn't know what to expect.

When my daughter Janna came to the hospital, she encouraged Janise to visit Aimee with her. Janna escorted Janise in a wheelchair to the neonatal ICU, offering her support during this heart-wrenching moment. I watched from a distance as Janise approached the bassinette. Leaning over, she quietly picked Aimee up, kissed her, and began to sob. We cried with her.

This was her baby, the baby they said was so disabled, and yet Aimee was alert and visibly happy to be in her mother's arms. It was a truly emotional reunion for mother and child. Later, Janise shared her recollections of that moment with me and how she was overwhelmed with dismay and disbelief the first time she held Aimee. She was afraid to see her and wondered if she would look normal. Janise also feared her own reactions; she had been told that Aimee was unresponsive. But when she held Aimee, all her fears went away and there was an immediate connection between them. Janise felt at peace and knew in some way that everything would work out.

· · ·

Sunday morning arrived quickly, and Janise and the twins were released to go home. Aimee's stay was uneventful and, fortunately, devoid of problems. The last item on the agenda for Aimee was a hearing test, but the results were inconclusive.

My throat tightened as I watched them drive away, the two car seats side by side in the backseat of the car. I wondered what the future would hold. At that moment, I reaffirmed my personal commitment to become as involved as possible. My role as grandmother was unknown to me then, and my journey into the future a mystery, but I knew with certainty that I loved these two little girls and would always be there for them.

FAMILY REFLECTIONS

FAMILY IS SO IMPORTANT IN OUR LIVES. Our faith in God and love of family embrace and support us in our time of need. This was the well from which I drew my strength. But a deep connection to these babies was a feeling I didn't anticipate. What I had expected, and what I now felt, were two different things. I was looking forward to the joy and "fun" of being a grandmother, but only from a safe distance that kept my life as I knew it then—my successful business, happy marriage, many friends, and very active social life—as it was.

My life was rich with experiences. I had traveled the world. Our four grown children had graduated from college and were pursuing their own lives and careers. Grandchildren would be part of my life but certainly not all-encompassing. My life was fulfilling already. I had often listened patiently as friends who were grandparents shared stories about their adorable grandkids. "Yeah, yeah," I thought.

But now everything was different. What now? What kind of grandmother would I be now that things were not as I had foolishly imagined? What new responsibilities would I have? My feelings ran deep and I tried to dissect what it was that frightened me. Was it Aimee, and what would happen to her? Was it Chloe, and her life without the companionship of her twin sister? Was it concern for my son and daughter-in-law, coping with the "cards that had been dealt," as my son often said? I decided to draw strength from the example of my own parents.

Everyone loved Connie and Domenic, or "Nuna" and "Nunu," as they were affectionately known to their grandchildren. Her name should have been the Italian "Nonna," not Nuna, but Ron, the first grandchild, couldn't quite get it. So it was Nuna to him and every grandchild thereafter. Connie had seven grandchildren, two step-grandchildren, and six great-grandchildren, including two sets of twin girls born three weeks apart, and she loved them all with a passion. She actively participated in their lives until her death in 1999 from cancer at age eighty. The children always wanted to go to Nuna's house and anticipated the treats she would offer and the time she spent with them because they all loved her. Now, I looked to her as a model as I struggled with my new role of grandmother.

• • •

I remembered her actions a thousand times over in the days and years that followed the twins' birth. My mother's life had not been easy. At age eight, Connie experienced the devastating and unexpected loss of her mother from an undiagnosed illness, which filled her life with sorrow. Because she never experienced the camaraderie of a mother-daughter relationship, she hadn't developed certain parenting skills that came easily for others. Connie often felt insecure and at a disadvantage regarding her own role as a mother. Nevertheless, her faith and optimism in every aspect of life provided an example for me now.

Shopping, planning parties, sharing secrets—she missed out on all the things girls normally do with their mothers but still tried her best to provide those activities for my sister and me. As the eldest daughter in her own family, she was strapped with the responsibility of caring for siblings along with managing all the other heavy chores expected of a farm girl growing up in what was then called the Valley of Hearts' Delight—now Silicon Valley. Her childhood was filled with duties that often kept her from attending school. She loved learning and was a good student but was never able to fulfill her dream of becoming a teacher.

The light in her childhood, the person she loved most in the world, was her maternal grandmother, who provided Connie with love, affection, encouragement, and a sense of self-worth. She remained a mentor to Connie throughout her life. Her grandmother was the only one who loved and never abandoned her daughter's motherless children, and she was the one person on whom Connie would base her own foundation of love and motherhood. Because of her, Connie grew into a woman of strength, resolve, and character.

• • •

My father came from Italy in 1916, when he was twelve, to fish in Alaska with his father. Because of a series of financial setbacks and a pregnant wife ready to give birth in Italy, my grandfather had to return home. When they separated, my father was instructed to remain in America with an older cousin until the entire family could return. But that never happened. His family remained in Italy, while he, still only a child, remained alone in America. Because of this early loss, family meant everything to my father.

Domenic was a man of exceptional integrity and high standards, especially in matters of respect, honor, and dignity. Volatile and tough on the surface, he was a gentle, deeply emotional man inside. His mother was only fifteen when he was born and she felt a special bond with him—her first-born son. Later to be separated from him forever, his mother remained in Domenic's heart all his life.

Domenic's father traveled abroad during much of his childhood, and when he wasn't at his mother's side, he spent most of his youth with his paternal grandfather. Once in America, he never saw his grandfather again; however, he did manage to see his parents just once more in his life, thirty-five years later. Although his time with his parents and grandfather was brief, Domenic used those relationships to mold his own character as a father. Sadly, he never knew Aimee and Chloe; he died in 1992 at age eighty-seven.

• • •

I believed that faith would see me through my darkest moments. I understood that it was my parents' example of courage, responsibility, and commitment that helped me, in turn, teach my son Jason the extraordinary fortitude, determination, and love that he exhibited with his own infant daughter in her time of need.

During these difficult days, I thought a lot about my parents. Domenic and Connie always put their family first, often sacrificing and doing without so that their children could experience what they had not. They were not perfect, but they always did their best. It was obvious they were more comfortable as grandparents than they had been as parents. Their affection and love for their grandchildren was boundless; they babysat, attended school performances, drove children to and from lessons, and organized countless craft and cooking projects. No effort was spared. My brother and sister both lived out of town or out of state for a number of years; even so, their children were never left out. Traveling across the state—or across the country—for visits, my parents packed favorite foods, books, and toys, and devoted energy solely to the grandchildren when they arrived.

I miss the family gatherings and Sunday dinners with my parents, siblings, nieces, and nephews. Now, looking back, I can appreciate more than ever how important those family gatherings were. With lively discussions, lots of noise, and huge meals, those afternoons developed confidence and character in us and in our children. Each child was recognized as an integral and important part of the family unit, with unique expectations and responsibilities.

My mother, in her own simple way, made each grandchild feel like the most important child in the world. When Connie died, every one of her grandchildren was positive that he or she had been her favorite. And each of them was right: While sorting out her possessions, we found scrapbooks and boxes containing every drawing, note, and card that her grandchildren had ever given her.

My parents were special. How would my grandparenting abilities compare to theirs? I would have to make some serious changes in my own life to live up to their example. I had a long way to go.

THE FIRST YEAR

CHAPTER 3

ONCE THE TWINS WERE HOME from the hospital things became hectic. The first two weeks were torture. Recovering from her C-section was painful for Janise, so Jackie came to San Jose to help. Jason had to return to work, clearly depressed in spite of trying hard to keep his life in balance. One or the other of the twins cried continuously throughout the night; it was more often Aimee who would cry and cry. Feeding times during the day seemed never-ending. A string of visitors came and went from the small condo, and the telephone rang nonstop. Everyone was exhausted and sleep deprived. By the end of the first week we had all reached our personal limits.

Having a new baby, or babies, should be a festive, joyous, and happy time. Instead, for us, it was overshadowed. We all experienced a spectrum of often opposing feelings: happiness and sadness, confidence and doubt, joy and sorrow, anger and fear, frustration and disappointment. No doubt the babies reacted to the uncertainty as well.

We tried to stay connected to and supportive of our children and each other, but life had to go on. We all had personal responsibilities that required our attention. Neglecting to plan for the worst, we were naïve to think life would continue as before. But who could have planned for this? From this point forward, we knew everything had changed, no matter how much we wanted to think otherwise.

. . .

I returned to work after a few days. My clients and employees were counting on me for direction and leadership. Luckily, my business was located just a few blocks from my son's condominium in downtown San Jose. There was no point in mourning forever.

On Thursday morning of the first week, I thought a mid-morning break might be nice for Janise and Jackie and brought them some scones and coffee cake from a local bakery. When I arrived, I was stunned at the situation. Both babies were crying their heads off. Janise and Jackie, in tears as well, were frustrated and exhausted. They hadn't eaten or slept and looked terrible. The place was in shambles and they clearly needed some rest.

I suggested they go to my house, where it was quiet, so that they could get some much-needed sleep. My offer was immediately accepted and they left within minutes. I was exhausted, too, when they came back a few hours later. Taking care of newborn twins is a challenge under normal circumstances; handling Aimee put us all on edge. We didn't know what we could or could not do and we were afraid of doing something that would hurt her even more.

The first months were unbearably difficult for everyone. Depressed, stressed, and exhausted, Jason and Janise now had unexpected financial complications to handle. Janise would not be able to return to work as previously planned, so Jason would be the sole means of support for his family. Mel and I decided to help by offering our guesthouse, rent free, as their residence as long as they wanted to stay. It was small but comfortable and we could modify a storage room into a nursery so the twins would have their own room. It had a small kitchen, living room, and loft bedroom, all furnished and stocked with linens and household items. They didn't really need to bring anything except themselves, their personal items, and all the things for the babies. In turn, they could sublet their condominium for extra income. They accepted the offer and moved in the following month.

The guesthouse was not attached to the main house. Our backyard, which we never used, was the front entry of the guesthouse, so they had their privacy. We had a large front yard with a swimming pool and courtyard, so we had privacy as well. They could come and go as they wished without disturbing us, and vice versa. We enjoyed having them so close and everyone settled in nicely. But the challenges were just beginning.

I spent much of that first year reading every piece of literature I could find on cerebral palsy and microcephaly. I talked with physicians and health professionals and learned all I could. One day Mario came to my office with news. "Matsu, you won't believe what I found on the Internet!" he said. He eagerly provided me with the name and telephone number of a man who had organized a microcephaly chat room and website. More than anything else this discovery opened the door to communicating directly with other families who had children with cerebral palsy and microcephaly. Maybe they could help us.

I learned that these children all had different symptoms and varying degrees of cerebral palsy. I also learned that all the parents felt like we did—hungry and desperate for information. I shared the information with Janise, and although she was interested, she thought it was too painful for her to participate. She asked me to get involved on her behalf.

• • •

Lesson one was an eye-opener: The parents seemed to share the sentiment that the doctors didn't know everything and that they could learn more by communicating directly with each other. This turned out to be absolutely true, and I was grateful for a connection that provided me with so much direction. Being a part of this community helped me stay positive.

I spent hours at my computer, reading questions and responses posted by parents from around the country. I often printed their stories for Janise to read. The information was pertinent, but it was frightening to learn from other families' experiences about the path we would travel with Aimee. Astonished that these concerned parents were so open and generous in sharing their heart-wrenching stories, Mel and I often cried together while reading them.

Jason heard none of it. I felt it was simply too painful for him to hear what the future would, or could, hold. Jason was not taking things well. I thought he was moody, argumentative, and perhaps in denial. He was not comfortable in any situation, social or otherwise, where he would be asked questions or had to discuss Aimee. I left it up to Janise to share what she wanted with him in their private moments.

The website, however, offered a significant avenue with which to connect and communicate with other families who felt the same fears and anxieties about their precious children as we did about Aimee. In time, Janise began to ask me to post questions for her. We would read the responses together, often crying, sometimes laughing, but always feeling more confident about our direction. Others confirmed what we had felt. Everything the physicians said was not always the truth or written in stone. We were encouraged by the other families to keep the faith, remain positive, and trust our intuition. But sometimes it was hard.

The toughest part of that difficult first year was when I accompanied Janise to Aimee's doctor appointments and diagnostic procedures. Each seemed more depressing than the last. A second test of Aimee's hearing also proved inconclusive. This was one of those times when we trusted our intuition that she, in fact, could hear. A pediatric ophthalmologist examined her and told us she would probably not be able to see. "Aimee has the equipment, but her optic nerves are severely damaged," the doctor said. "Think of it as telephone equipment that can work but that is not connected to the telephone pole."

A return visit to the pediatric neurologist at three months was discouraging as well. We left infuriated at his comments that there was nothing that could be done for Aimee. "The parents need to accept it," he said, without compassion. Six months later, a different pediatric neurologist, with a kinder bedside manner, told Janise that if Aimee ever recognized her it would be a major accomplishment. His words stung like arrows. Janise, in tears, was shocked and heartbroken. The sadness and disappointment in her eyes brought me to an all-time low. The doctor said there would be little, if anything, Aimee would be capable of doing, but he encouraged us nevertheless to do our best with her because no one really knew for sure. A follow-up MRI at age one concluded that there was no change in the status of her brain. The prognosis remained grim.

In spite of the consistent negativity from the collective medical world, we continued to feel that Aimee was more responsive than doctors said she would be. She related to us and we believed she could hear and see shadows and movement. Loud noises startled her and she would turn her head and look in the direction of someone speaking or making noise. We ignored the negative and continued to treat Aimee and Chloe the same.

Everyone who visited Chloe and Aimee treated them the same way—held them, talked to them, and loved them. When Aimee would cry in fear, or startle in response to a sound, she was reassured with hugs, kisses, and cuddles. Although she remained smaller than Chloe, she ate well and thrived, a positive sign of her strength—as was the fact that Aimee demanded her share of attention even as she fell developmentally farther and farther behind Chloe.

When Chloe was cooing in response to sounds and stimuli, Aimee would become frightened and jumpy. When Chloe was sitting up and beginning to crawl, Aimee did neither. When Chloe began to speak, Aimee remained silent. But beyond the silence, we sensed that Aimee very much wanted to communicate with us. It was clear that she was responsive to human contact and wanted to share in the loving relationships that surrounded her.

• • •

One day Janise thought Aimee smiled. When Aimee smiled again the next day, Janise told me about it. Aimee appeared to enjoy soothing and repetitive sounds, words, phrases, and stories. The first time she smiled at me, I was telling her the alphabet. I often repeated the ABCs. I would begin in a singsong tone of "Aaaaaaaaaaa, Beeeeeeeeee, and C!" over and over.

Aimee listened and anticipated my tone and cadence. Finally one day she smiled! "Oh my God!" I shouted, "She smiled."

More important, she had *responded.* We had no doubt that she was actually smiling and communicating. When I repeated the same A-B-C phrase several times over, just to be sure, she smiled again and again. I ran to the guesthouse, overjoyed, to share my excitement with Janise. "Oh, Janise, this is so important," I said. "She has the ability to respond and to interact with us! This is a major breakthrough!" That moment, that day, was the first of many such experiences that made us determined not to give up on this precious little girl.

• • •

Among their other dire predictions, the doctors had said that Aimee would not live past one year. When her first year came to an end and she was alive and thriving, I wanted to celebrate in a big way. I had been consoled and comforted by so many family members and friends during that first year that I wanted to share my appreciation and joy with them. My husband had been particularly patient and supportive. He cried and prayed with me often; a party would do us all good.

I talked with Jason and Janise and expressed my desire to host a birthday party for the twins and invite everyone who had been there for us this first year. They agreed, and I happily got to work planning the invitations, menu, and entertainment to reflect a circus theme. It was a wonderful event attended by family and friends and lots of children.

When it was time to cut cake, Aimee and Chloe each had a small cake placed in front of them. Aimee touched and smashed the cake and put it to her face. Once she tasted it, she wanted to taste more. Of course, Chloe dug in as only a typical one-year-old can. Aimee was having fun until everyone began to sing "Happy Birthday." Startled, she began to scream and cry. As she cried, everyone present embraced this celebration of life.

It was fitting that this little girl, thought to be deaf, blind, and doomed, was crying because she could hear—she was participating the only way she knew. She had defied the odds and made it.

The Path of Change

AIMEE WAS ALIVE. She had defied all odds and made it through her first year. Her obvious will to live gave me optimism and hope for the coming year. And I was going to need every bit of it. Torn between my commitment to my family and business responsibilities, I tried desperately to free up time to help with the twins and, in particular, Aimee. My years of experience in the health industry and the fact that my husband is a health professional helped Janise navigate the medical jargon. But I knew I could be of even more help. If I were to continue helping with Aimee, I definitely felt I needed to hear doctor's reports firsthand. Establishing time in my busy schedule to help Janise with the children was almost impossible, and the coming year would bring a series of devastating personal events that I couldn't have imagined.

In early 1998, our recently renovated second home, located on the California coast, was ruined by smoke damage from an adjoining unit that had burned to the ground. We had to remove, repair, or replace everything we owned. It was six months before we were able to move back in.

Business stresses were also taking a toll on me. The medical billing field was in a state of unprecedented change, which was hurting my company's bottom line, and I was forced to downsize. I purchased a small storefront building from which to operate and moved out of a downtown high-rise building. My downsizing was not only a sound business decision at the time but a good personal one as well. After working sixty-hour weeks for years, my priorities had now changed. In addition to wanting time to spend with Aimee, I was burned out and longed for a career change. The new location allowed me to open a small antiques and home accessory shop in the front part of the building, while operating my medical billing company in back.

I was excited about this new course, and it took eight months to implement these changes. Key to the plan was a trusted and dependable employee who had worked for me for more than eleven years. She would remain in charge of the billing company, now easily manageable, in exchange for a percentage of ownership. We would move to a 1,000-square-foot temporary location for six months, while the new storefront was renovated. I would finally be able to take more personal time off. It was perfect.

On Monday of the week we were scheduled to move to the temporary location, I was hit with a shocking and unexpected blow. My long-time, esteemed employee failed to show up for work. Her desk and office were empty. There was none of the usual office paraphernalia; important client files and financial records were gone. When I tried to call her, I discovered her phone was disconnected. She had moved out of her house and left no forwarding information. I was devastated and completely numb.

I spent weeks and months poring over records, documents, and computer reports. More and more financial discrepancies unfolded and had to be documented. I was furious at first, and then I blamed myself. My integrity was impeccable and I had always sought to keep it that way. When the situation became more complicated, lawyers and accountants were called in. It took many months and tens of thousands of dollars to sort it all out.

I was stressed to the maximum but remained as strong as I could in the face of this disastrous situation. I had paid a huge price professionally, financially, and emotionally, but in the interest of moving on with my life, I decided that I simply didn't have the energy or resources for continued litigation and that ruminating over the situation for months to come would only add more stress to my already complicated life. For my own sake and well-being, I needed to let go of my anger and move on. Forgiveness was the wiser choice for me and undeniably in keeping with my personal values; through it, I could finally experience closure. It proved to be a good decision in the end.

Aimee gave me focus and resolve during this tough time. Seeing her smile was a joy beyond words. Her obvious desire to communicate and interact was contagious and I longed to spend more time with her and Chloe. I tried to help by taking one of the twins for an hour or so each day after work. Usually it was Aimee. She would sit in her special adaptive chair, placed on the kitchen table, and watch as Mel and I went about our tasks. We talked and played with her or fed and bathed her. Her baths were best done in our divided kitchen sink, where we could prop her against the sides and hold her at the same time.

Mel, full of love and support, took it upon himself to fill in for me when I wasn't available. He helped with the twins and did the shopping for Janise and me. We all tried to do our best to take things one day at a time. Jason needed support, too, and was doing his best to cope. He managed their personal finances and focused on his responsibilities at work, but, deep down, I felt that he was struggling with the reality of the situation.

That holiday season passed in a blur. Too busy and too depressed to decorate for Christmas, I simply put lights and ribbons on the tree. Unpacking the ornaments and decorating was a luxury of time and mental energy I could not afford. Every holiday season, without fail, I bake, decorate, and entertain to the hilt. Not that year.

My brother, sister, and I planned an eightieth birthday party for our mother. This was another priority that required my time and attention. In retrospect, it was the most important thing I could have done at the time, and I'm grateful I did. I had no idea it would be my mother's last birthday.

During that time, I served on the Board of Directors of Via Rehabilitation Services in Santa Clara. One day, I was asked to visit their Early Start Center. I had no sense of the work they did with special-needs children under the age of three. Observing the compassion, patience, and kindness of the staff interacting with the parents and children brought me to tears. I had to hide my face when I joined their "circle time." I was truly amazed as each child, in turn, was encouraged to select an item that the group would sing about. I had never spent time around disabled children and I was astonished that they were actually capable of accomplishing this task. I left with a heavy heart but one filled with inspiration at the remarkable interaction I had observed that day.

Aimee, now one and a half, still did not have the strength to sit independently; however, she could be propped up and strapped into her special high chair. The spasticity that would get worse as she grew had not yet set in. She was "flexible" and not stiff, although still not fully coordinated. An occupational therapist came weekly to work with her on different movements and skills, such as bringing her hands together and to her mouth. The teaching methods were simple but ingenious. Chocolate pudding was used as an incentive—Aimee would touch, taste, and then bring her fingers to her mouth to taste again. What child wouldn't want another taste of chocolate pudding?

One day, Janise asked me to accompany her to Aimee's first class for very young special-needs children. She told me that the program was at the Via Rehabilitation facility. When we arrived, I was completely surprised to see it was the same place I had visited months earlier. It was a pleasure to now observe Janise share her experiences and discuss common problems and concerns with other parents in similar situations. Some of the children seemed to be in worse shape than Aimee. We were grateful that Aimee appeared alert and didn't have to be heavily medicated. Unfortunately, many children with seizures remain in a state of near unconsciousness because of their medication.

The experience, while sobering, helped us appreciate Aimee's limited abilities all the more. No matter how bad we felt, we learned there were others who suffered more. It gave us both a sense of perspective.

And for Janise, it was confirmation of sorts that she was not alone in her fears or her pain.

When Janise could not attend the classes, she asked me to take Aimee. I thoroughly enjoyed participating with her. During these sessions, I began to observe her very intently. She had good comprehension of the activities and anticipated certain tasks and games. For example, she liked singing songs in the group circle, but she cried in fright when she anticipated clapping at the end of each song.

At the conclusion of each session, the kids could play outside. Although these kids were unable to run to the swings, climb the slides, or jump on the equipment, they knew what was happening. Teachers and parents wheeled or carried them to the playground. Then the fun began. To my amazement the kids communicated their excitement in a variety of ways, through body language, grunts, smiles, screams, or tears. I began to understand that these children, although disabled, were no different from normal children in their need and desire to play with others and enjoy the world around them. Aimee especially enjoyed the slide and the swing. When she smiled, I smiled too, because I knew she was having fun.

I began to understand Aimee in a different way. Movement and sound frightened her, but with patience, encouragement, and trust, she would allow us to introduce her to new experiences, one at a time. Mel and I began to take Aimee and Chloe to local parks, where they could play together. Aimee's first experience on the carousel was frightening for her. She was stiff and rigid as the music and movement began, and it was extremely difficult to hold her on the horse. But persistence prevailed, and she learned that the ride had a beginning and an end. Chloe often helped diminish her fear when she laughed at her sister. We chanted "up," "down," "up," "down" until she felt the rhythm. Her confidence grew and finally, slowly, she began to enjoy the ride.

Aimee could overcome her fears through trust. She trusted me completely. I took this seriously and understood that her trust was never to be betrayed or compromised. That trust became the foundation of our relationship. With encouragement I could expand on opportunities for Aimee she would otherwise never experience.

THE UNEXPECTED MOVE

WE WERE COMFORTABLE and enjoyed having the kids in our guesthouse. It was an arrangement that seemed to work for everyone. I wish I could have provided more help to Janise in the day-to-day care of the twins. I knew she was overwhelmed, and I was, too, but for different reasons. Everything came to a head one afternoon when I returned home from a difficult day at work. Janise needed help, but I needed to prepare some documents for a legal meeting the following morning with a large medical group. "You're never available when I need you!" Janise yelled. "I feel stuck here all day, without help, and you're always too busy to do anything of significance to help me out!"

Her fury was directed at me alone and I was shocked by her vehemence. I wrongly assumed she understood my business responsibilities and contractual obligations. I couldn't jeopardize my company, my clients, or employees. They depended on me too.

"Janise, give me a break!" I shouted. "I've done everything I could possibly do to help and have opened my home for you in every possible way." I was devastated by her anger at me. Surprisingly, she was not angry with Mel. He had been more accessible, but it wasn't his help she needed, it was mine. But I had nothing left. I understood that her indignation, resentment, and heartbreak ran deep, and I knew it wasn't just about me but about the entire situation. Although we moved past it, this flash point on the surface created a wedge in our relationship in subtle ways in the months that followed. I knew how she felt, but there was nothing I could do to make things different.

Four weeks later, Jason told us they would be moving to Modesto, where Janise had grown up and her family still lived. I had had a feeling that Janise's anger displayed weeks earlier would end this way. Janise felt isolated and alone. Jason had to do what was best for his wife and family, even if it meant changing jobs and moving away from his own family and friends. He was prepared to make the sacrifice.

They left the following weekend. I cried for two days and Mel cried right along with me. He adored having the children here and thoroughly enjoyed every moment with them. Nevertheless, they were leaving, and there was nothing else we could do but wish them well. The time it took to drive back and forth to Modesto, about ninety minutes each way, was clearly going to present a hardship. They remained close enough to visit, just not as often as we would have preferred. We counted our blessings, and I made up my mind that, one way or another, I would make it work. I vowed to visit them once a week.

That was when my mother was diagnosed with terminal cancer. It was another shock. She had been in excellent health all her life. During the last ten years my mother had worked with me at my billing company. She was a dynamo at her job. She loved the independent lifestyle it provided after a lifetime spent as a homemaker. She was proud of the fact that, in her senior years, she had become a "career woman," entirely supporting herself.

The doctors offered chemotherapy and told us that it was only a matter of time; they said there wasn't anything else they could do. My mother wanted every chance available to help her live as long as possible and proceeded with the chemotherapy. She lived within a mile of my home and naturally expected that I would take her to her daily treatments. Her health-care needs grew, and soon she could not provide for herself; the family gathered to establish her care plan. Every grandchild wanted to help and each assumed responsibility for cooking meals and staying overnight with her at her home during the week. My brother, sister, and I would rotate and assume responsibility for weekend care.

Spring and summer flew by. It was a very, very depressing time for me—probably the most depressing time of my life. My business remained in crisis, I missed my son and his family, and my mother was fighting cancer and clearly losing the battle. Her fear of dying was palpable and she cried each time she had to endure another chemotherapy session. I wanted to be with her as much as I could, even if it was only to console her and sit by her side. Every minute counted; there was so little time left.

Janise and Jason visited her regularly. During these visits my mother loved to see the twins. As sick as she was, she would hold Chloe on her lap and read to her just as she had done with every other grandchild. She would also hold Aimee and talk to her as one would an infant; she would call her "poor thing," feeling sorry for what had happened to her.

• • •

The twins celebrated their second birthday at a beautiful park in Modesto. As usual, lots of family and friends came to the barbeque and celebration. Like all kids, the twins loved the park. Chloe headed straight for the playground equipment. Aimee wanted to swing, too, which required being held on someone's lap. Consequently, our gift to the twins that year was a swing set with a special adaptive swing for Aimee. We had vowed in the beginning to always treat Aimee and Chloe equally, and that commitment was becoming more and more difficult to maintain. But the swing set was the perfect gift for both girls, and Aimee could swing independently in her special seat.

Although very ill from the effects of cancer and chemotherapy, my mother insisted on attending the party. She had lost her hair and appetite. Her head was covered in a wrap and the heat became unbearable for her even in the shade. It was one of those hot, triple-digit, record-temperature days, but she refused to leave and insisted on taking part in the festivities. Perhaps she knew it would be her final family gathering. It was the last day any photographs of her were taken.

My mother passed away in her home, with her family at her side, six weeks later. Children, grandchildren, and great-grandchildren alike mourned this loving woman who had sacrificed so much for her family. During our final hours together she praised and encouraged me to continue to help Aimee in whatever way possible. Longing for times past when I could ask her guidance, I now felt a deep void where her opinion would have been shared. I miss her terribly.

• • •

Another holiday season was quickly approaching. I was thankful for the twins in my life and renewed my commitment to make Christmas the best I could under the circumstances just as my mother would have done. In spite of my sorrow and other hardships, I was managing to endure. Aimee was alive and thriving. I had much to be thankful for.

I prayed that the New Year would bring renewed hope and focus to my life. It was the millennial year and an inspirational time to reflect on my life and future goals. I intended to sell my medical billing business during the coming year. I had entertained the notion for some time and had no specific scheme to accomplish this goal, but I knew it had to be done. My desire to help Aimee was a priority that gave me direction. I regretted many things I could have done differently as a mother. Now, as a grandmother, I didn't want to regret any further missed opportunities.

The year had been difficult. Doctor visits had provided little, if any, new information about Aimee's condition. I continued to accompany Janise to appointments with a variety of specialists, where each consultation ended with the same doom-and-gloom prognosis and made me more determined than ever to learn how to help Aimee. I just could not accept the reality those doctors presented. Janise and I were not about to give up or leave any stone unturned. She and Aimee had my full commitment and support; I would do all I possibly could.

• • •

When she was two, Aimee discovered the world of TV and video. With her limited vision but keen hearing, her desire for music always reigned supreme. Elmo and *Sesame Street* characters became her friends and idols, not because she saw them but because she *heard* them. We knew that she recognized Elmo when she saw him, probably because he was bright red. She would grin at songs she recognized. When she was sitting on my lap, I would tell her to "feel" the beat and help her clap her hands together in time with the music.

One physician along the way suggested that Aimee listen to "quiet and soothing" music to develop her brain. So we did that, but soon Aimee was bored with classical music. Instead, she loved a rock-and-roll beat, especially Elvis. She would listen for hours, not only to Elvis but to any music that rocked.

Through music, Aimee learned to demonstrate her preferences and took obvious pleasure in being understood. This was a clear indication that she was beginning to develop some social skills. Her potential to relate and respond to others and to her surroundings had become not just a possibility but a reality.

Books also expanded her world. She enjoyed being read to and reached out to touch the pages. Did she see the images on the pages? We didn't know, but she apparently saw some of it. Her favorite books and stories were always about Elmo. When she reached out to touch the pages as I read, I wondered if it was the colored images or the actual paper that interested her. Aimee began to use facial expressions and body language to communicate her likes and dislikes about music, books, and toys.

If she liked something, she would smile and reach out; but if she disliked it, her face would show it all. She would frown and her body would become rigid. We may have been the ones learning to communicate with her, rather than the other way around, but we were able to communicate nevertheless, which meant that we could offer Aimee a variety of activities we knew she would enjoy.

I observed Aimee closely, trying to analyze her in every way. Developmentally, she was trailing behind Chloe—yet she also progressed because of Chloe. The twins loved to play together and audio-related entertainment was something they could share.

Chloe's influence on Aimee has always been profound and very positive. Perhaps without her sister, Aimee would not be as strong. Chloe would jump and run around the room doing her own thing, while Aimee passively observed. But she absorbed what was going on. Sometimes Chloe would act silly to get Aimee to respond, and when Aimee would kick her legs trying to imitate what Chloe was doing they would laugh together and Chloe would give her a big hug.

To be sure, Aimee's progress had to be measured in bits and pieces, but she had come a long way. Considering what we were told by the doctors—that Aimee would never be capable of hearing, seeing, or responding—she had already surpassed their predictions. Clearly, Aimee's home environment played a big role in her early development. And this constant social stimulation with adults and children encouraged Aimee's participation in her preschool program.

Aimee's strong character began to reveal itself early on. For example, if a visitor entered the room and greeted everyone else and ignored Aimee, she made it known she was there, too, and didn't like being overlooked one bit! She expressed herself through loud moans and other sounds until she was acknowledged. Although she didn't speak, she did communicate.

Aimee became a familiar figure to our circle of friends. To our surprise, she would remember the people she met weeks, even months, later. We believed it was her keen sense of hearing that helped her recognize these individuals. Perhaps it was each person's unique tone or accent, but once that person spoke, she remembered who it was immediately. Small mental tasks that might appear simple to others were monumental for Aimee, so displays of recognition were tremendous steps—steps that were important indicators that she could live beyond a "vegetative state." But her progress was slow.

Chloe's development progressed at a normal rate, and it was painful to see Aimee falling further and further behind. Aimee startled at unfamiliar sounds and became frightened and anxious in any new situation. Parties, parades, noisy pizza parlors, clapping, and shopping often put her over the top. A new toy with any type of metallic sound, flashing lights, or awkward shape could cause a meltdown of extreme proportions, making it impossible to reintroduce that toy later. Aimee remembered every unpleasant experience, and anticipating a repeat of those experiences would leave her overcome with anxiety and fear.

Janise often asked me to take Aimee for the day, or weekend, so that the rest of the family could enjoy social occasions or activities that Aimee could not tolerate. I encouraged Aimee's participation in family activities; however, in all fairness, sometimes it was nice for everyone else to be able to enjoy an occasion without being completely absorbed in calming Aimee.

Jason and Janise had complete trust in Mel and me regarding Aimee's care. We were familiar with her equipment and how to use it, understood her needs, and enjoyed her companionship. Aimee's spirit has always moved me very deeply, and Mel and I experienced it most clearly when she stayed with us. Working quietly one-on-one with Aimee so that she could focus on learning something new revealed her strong desire to learn and her ability to recall information.

Now almost three, unable to sit, crawl, or walk, Aimee had a special-needs chair for feeding and mobility. There was a lot we all had to learn: special-needs catalogs displayed complicated equipment including adaptive standers, chairs, strollers, walkers, wheelchairs, and toys. Pictures of equipment designed to aid and enrich the child's physical and mental development were overwhelming. We had no doubt that Aimee would require these items as she grew and knew it was only a matter of time before she would need a regular wheelchair, perhaps for life.

THE BREAKTHROUGH

A STROLLER AND AN ADAPTIVE CHAIR had met Aimee's needs in the past. But now that she was getting bigger and unable to sit up or walk independently, Aimee's therapists recommended that we get a wheelchair for her. She was fitted, and the chair was finally delivered; but even so, the thought that she was destined to spend her life in a wheelchair made everyone gloomy.

Janise called me from Modesto, sobbing. "Aimee's new wheelchair is here and it's so small," she said. She couldn't say more. I understood her tears and why she was crying. I tried to comfort her but was in tears myself. I drove to Modesto the following day to see it for myself. It truly was sad. For us, this little contraption meant the end of our dream that Aimee would walk someday.

It seemed unreal to me to see our darling little girl, only three years old and so small, strapped in a chair. It was a sophisticated chair—small in scale but appropriate in every detail and functionality. In it, and with the support of a butterfly harness across her chest, Aimee could sit up straight. A strap secured her tightly at the waist and her feet were strapped on footplates. She was smiling and happy, but I cried at my first sight of her bound to the chair. Still, I knew it would help her and Janise by providing the mobility so needed for her care.

It also would provide a means by which she could ride the bus to preschool. A tray attached to the front of the chair served as a desktop for schoolwork and a tabletop for feeding. From that day forward, her wheelchair went everywhere with her. It would become an important part of her existence—not only for her care, but also as an extension of Aimee herself.

• • •

Late one summer evening, Janise phoned, sounding anxious and excited. "Turn on the TV," she said. "There's a program I want you to see." It was about an innovative physical therapy regimen in Poland for children with cerebral palsy and other debilitating conditions. The therapy had helped some children to walk and offered possibilities for other areas of improvement.

The idea involved concepts of patterning, physical therapy, and something we didn't know about called *Adeli suit* therapy. Janise was enthusiastic about what she had seen. I, too, was curious about the therapy and found it very interesting. I wondered if it was something that could help Aimee. I thought about it a lot. But how in the world would we get Aimee to Poland? I didn't think Janise, despite her interest, would allow it. And I knew Jason never would.

I was wrong. Days later, I was astonished when Janise asked me if I would ever consider doing something like the Polish program with Aimee. "Yes!" I replied, without hesitation. But first, we would have to learn more about it and determine whether the benefits would help her. My friend, Mario Cordero, the doctor who had offered so much support in the past, now volunteered to look into it, using his resources at the hospital library. Weeks later, he came to me and said he had found information on Euromed and the Adeli suit. The rehabilitation center had opened in 1994. I was able to contact Euromed in Poland and obtain information about the program from them. I was also given the name of a contact person in the United States. It was time for me to do some research.

I located a website that provided information about the *Adeli Project*, which explained that the Adeli suit was originally designed in Russia to help cosmonauts adjust to low-gravity conditions and weightlessness in space. The idea is to move body parts against a resistance, thus improving muscle strength. In the 1990s it was developed as a mode of therapy for individuals, specifically children, with cerebral palsy. The suit is specially designed to correct the patient's posture and movements. To do that, it adjusts the course of the muscles, forcing them to move as closely as possible to the way they would if they functioned normally. By doing so, it apparently also affects the damaged centers of the brain responsible for motor and speech control. They say that therapy in the suit trains the brain to remember, through correct body alignment and patterning, how the muscles should move.

The suit is essentially a set of supporting units in the form of shoulder pads, a vest, shorts, knee pads, and shoes, which are connected to each other through a system of adjustable elastic ties or bands. It is possible to add additional bands to correct the alignment of the feet and shoulders and to adjust the bands to vary the patient's posture and limb position. The placement of the elastic bands determines the selected muscle groups that will be exercised as the patient moves; this therapy is a form of controlled resistance exercise. It maintains the correct posture and adjusts the course of movements. The suit is also supposed to increase physical endurance and improve coordination, acting as an exoskeleton framework.

While researching the Adeli suit, I learned that there was no scientific literature or studies to document the safety or effectiveness of the suit therapy for treatment of cerebral palsy. I kept investigating. I contacted three parents who had taken their children to Poland for the therapy. Although, they were very enthusiastic about the results, the therapy had not resulted in their children walking in every instance. One had actually been able to go from a wheelchair to a walker and another had gone from walking with crutches to walking independently for short periods of time. Both children still relied on a wheelchair for most of their mobility. I forwarded this information to Janise and suggested she contact these parents as well. She did so and was encouraged after talking with them.

The treatment is noninvasive but intense. Although there are some risks, it produces no harmful effects that we could see that would be likely to lead to deterioration of the patient's condition. We learned that the apparent benefits vary with each child. Depending on the severity of the cerebral palsy, improvement might be provided in several ways: retraining the nervous system, improvement of external stabilization, improving muscle tone, alignment of the body, improved balance, and improved coordination and support of weak muscles. Other benefits included improvement of spatial awareness; improved speech fluency through head, neck, and trunk support; and improvement of bone density to help decrease contractures (chronic shortening of muscles due to spasticity and abnormal tone that limits movement and motor ability). With these facts in mind, we determined that the possibility of improvement was greater than the risks involved. And it was better than doing nothing at all.

But it wasn't simple or cheap. First, we had to get to Poland—for four weeks. Cost was a big issue. The therapy was not covered by insurance, and travel expenses would have to be paid out of pocket. Time away from work meant loss of income for a month. Child care for Chloe during our absence was a major concern for Janise. I agreed to go along if Aimee were accepted, because Janise felt she could not make the trip alone. One way or another, we would manage expenses and make arrangements for Chloe. We proceeded with the application process.

In October of that year, the U.S. representative from Euromed contacted Janise. There was an unexpected cancellation and they had an immediate opening for Aimee if we could come in two weeks. We weren't expecting a response so soon and thought there would be more time to prepare. I couldn't leave my business on such short notice without reasonable preparation for my absence. We told them no.

Then, to my surprise and dismay, Janise confided that she was pregnant! This really complicated our plans. I was concerned about her traveling so far from home while pregnant. I didn't want to encourage her to make a trip that could lead to problems or complications, especially if she were pregnant with twins again—a very real possibility. But she definitely wanted to go and felt that if we waited, making the trip with a new baby would be impossible. We agreed that she would consult her physician first. I wasn't taking any unnecessary risks, no matter how much I wanted to help Aimee.

Euromed had another opening—this one for January. They would hold the reservation for two weeks, in which time we would have to make a decision. Therapy would have to be paid for in advance and there were no refunds. We estimated the entire cost to be around $12,000. If we wanted Aimee to have the therapy, January was the only time we would be able to go or we would have to wait another year or more. We decided to go for it.

• • •

Research complete, finances in line, child care for Chloe arranged, and medical documentation in order for Aimee, we were ready. Janise received permission from her physician to travel before the end of the second trimester. But then came an unexpected obstacle. My son didn't want us to go and pleaded with us to reconsider. He was angry with me and angry with Janise. Her pregnancy had made him believe that our trip to Poland would be forgotten. Certainly she wouldn't take such a risk, he thought. But Janise was determined to go; actually, her pregnancy escalated our desire to make the trip because of the travel constraints the airlines placed on pregnant women. Jason finally relented under pressure. He gave us his blessing, reluctantly.

Planning the trip was my responsibility and it was a major production. Four weeks before our departure, as was suggested, we shipped supplies and small quantities of food to Poland that we would need during our stay. The boxes would be there for us when we arrived. Poland was still considered a third world country, recently free from Communism. Conveniences were apparently few and far between.

43

We departed from San Francisco on New Year's Eve day, 2000. We flew to Chicago and connected with families who would fly to Warsaw with us. We didn't know anyone and had no expectations about what was to come.

Our departure was uneventful. Aimee had been excellent until the moment we boarded the airplane. She became anxious in the unfamiliar and enclosed surroundings. I had prepared her for traveling with some sound games to familiarize her with the routine announcements, bells, and buzzes she would hear on the plane. Sitting next to her, we played those games, and I was pleased when she began to smile and relax. Soon, she was fast asleep.

I considered myself a seasoned traveler and understood the benefits of packing light. But we still had a lot to handle: two carry-on bags, a diaper bag and small doll for Aimee, the wheelchair and tray, and a car seat for air travel. In addition, we had coats, hats, and scarves. We were given assistance through the security process and accompanied to the appropriate departure gate, located in a remote area of the airport.

The terminal was deserted and without signage. There we were— me, a pregnant woman, a handicapped child, and mounds of stuff— alone for over an hour. We even thought we might be at the wrong gate! Finally, we noticed a woman walking toward us with a young boy in a wheelchair. We had been assured that we would meet other families in Chicago. Our concerns diminished quickly and we were relieved when we knew we weren't alone.

One by one, other families arrived. First came a woman and her four-year-old son from Atlanta, who were making their second trip. Next was another woman who had driven from Detroit with her three-year-old daughter. This was their first trip. Soon, a tall, handsome man from Kentucky arrived with his thirteen-year-old son. This was their seventh trip to Euromed. A young girl from California and her parents, who were making their second trip, followed them. Harvey, and his son, Matthew, arrived loaded down with luggage and gear. They had made several trips to Poland. Last to arrive was an attractive woman, her mother-in-law, and her son, Brandon, who was around eight years old. Within fifteen minutes the empty terminal was filled with parents and children, bags and luggage, wheelchairs, and more special-needs equipment than you could imagine. These were the American families we would be living with for the next four weeks. Aimee was happy to see other children and greeted everyone with bright eyes and a big smile.

As we waited, I noticed that the kids immediately bonded and connected with each other; they seemed to be aware that they were alike. In many ways, they were no different from other children: impatient at waiting. The older kids were eager to get going and couldn't wait to board the plane. This was all new to Aimee. I was certain she didn't know what was going on, but she was happy simply being in the company of other kids.

My heart wrenched at the sight of them huddled in a circle, curious, and eager to meet each other. I thought of these children and their parents not with pity, but with hope—that one day the children would walk—because we, too, shared that dream. Tears filled my eyes as we lined up like a row of train cars to enter the plane. Aimee, the youngest of the children, sat in her tiny wheelchair. The sight of her, trapped in her chair, just like the big kids, brought reality home that this was to be her life and her world. These children, and children like them, would be her friends and classmates in the future. We had made it this far safely, and I was able to relax and get some rest. Our flight to Warsaw was comfortable. Aimee did great all the way.

In Warsaw, the weather was bitterly cold. I carried Aimee off the plane and down the steps to a waiting bus, where we were taken to the customs area. From there, we were bused to another terminal to board our flight to Szczecin, located in the northwest corner of Poland, near Germany, on the Baltic Sea.

We were finally on our last leg, in an old thirty-passenger plane. My heart was in my throat as the plane raced down the runway, rattling and jerking. I feared we wouldn't get off the ground. Then, suddenly, we were in the air. I held Aimee's little hand tight and said a prayer. It was a relatively short flight, and I hoped we would be safe.

A bus picked us up in Szczecin, for the more-or-less five-hour drive, heading east, to Mielno, Poland. It was late afternoon when we arrived and the children were hungry. We managed to stay awake for a couple of hours until dinner was served. We each ate a bowl of soup and went directly to bed. We had been on the road for more than thirty hours.

What awaited us was far from luxurious. Our room was clean, but mismatched linens and small worn bath towels added to the sub-standard feel. Our room was approximately 12 by 16 feet, including a small bathroom. The furnishings included two twin-sized beds with drawers under the mattress, a small sofa bed, a little square table and two chairs, a cabinet, and a small refrigerator. The room was dark and dull. Two rusted chairs were on the small balcony, which we could not use because of the cold weather and snow. Aimee adapted to her new surroundings without any problems. It was more difficult for Janise and me, but as we told each other, it would only be a month.

Medical evaluations for Aimee were scheduled on our second day. Although she had been prescreened, we still worried lest they find something that would prevent her from proceeding with therapy. One by one, the physicians examined Aimee, completed their evaluations, and provided direction to the therapists for her treatment. It was a relief when the evaluations were over and it was confirmed that Aimee would begin therapy the following day.

We were amazed that we were actually in Poland. And we were grateful that we were safe. It had been a long journey in more ways than one. We were ready to meet the challenges of the next four weeks.

POLAND

CHAPTER 7

NOW THAT AIMEE HAD COMPLETED her evaluations, we could begin to explore our surroundings. The dismal facility consisted of several post-WWII buildings capable of accommodating fifty to seventy patients and their families. The buildings were apparently owned by a foreign government and, by my standards, marginally maintained, adding to the winter gloom. Although connected via a variety of ramps, lifts, and elevators, making it possible to navigate internally from one building to another in cold weather, the facilities were operated by two different business entities: Euromed provided rehabilitation and therapy services, and Syrena managed the accommodations and food service. In addition to dormitory-style rooms, each building also housed patient therapy rooms and administrative offices. The reception and lobby area, kitchen and dining room, and large hospitality rooms were all located on the ground floor of what appeared to be the main building. A damp, stuffy, and steamy third-floor location housed a dated swimming pool, hot tub, sauna, and lockers, and the fenced and gated gardens consisted of patchy lawns, uneven paths of varying surfaces, and a small playground, all of which had suffered the consequences of winter weather. It was, in a word, depressing.

Mielno, a small charming coastal village dotted with restaurants and cafes, was much nicer than the facility. The village's markets and shops, although few, were within easy walking distance of the center. A beautiful expanse of beach bordered by a promenade running the length of the village's north side made for a nice walk, although not completely accessible by wheelchair. If we wanted to walk with Aimee from one end of the promenade to the other, we would have to exit on one street and return to the promenade from another location with a ramp a block away.

Main street ran along the south side of the village. Several parallel streets ran in an east-west direction, which made it fairly easy to briskly walk the entire village in half an hour in good weather. Mielno also had one Catholic church, a post office, two pharmacies, and a few kiosks selling a variety of food and miscellaneous items. Small hotels, apartments, old homes, and newer homes built following the demise of Communist rule provided an interesting variety of pre- and post-WWII architecture.

Transportation was limited to taxi or bus. Koszalin, about twenty-five minutes away, provided substantial shopping options for food, clothing, jewelry, and entertainment. The McDonald's in town was a favorite with the locals and foreigners alike, as was the Italian restaurant, Viva Italia.

Going anywhere, however, became a major production. First, it was freezing cold; second, maneuvering the wheelchair on icy sidewalks and streets was difficult and dangerous; and third, getting Aimee in and out of warm clothing made her bulky and took time. Travel by cab or bus was dependent on the availability of a vehicle that could accommodate a wheelchair. These challenges, along with Janise's pregnancy, almost made it easier to remain indoors and avoid the potential for an accident or illness.

On our first day at the center, Aimee was fitted for her Adeli suit, which would be used exclusively by her during her stay at Euromed. An English interpreter was assigned to us so that we could communicate with the physicians and therapy staff. The medical staff, available to us twenty-four hours a day, consisted of several doctors, a psychologist, a speech therapist, physical therapists, and nurses. The children were provided with complete medical care during their stay.

Symptoms of illness were immediately treated by a nurse and, if necessary, a doctor, so as not to infect or expose other children. A sick child would be isolated or confined to his or her room to eliminate the risk to others. Illness was a major concern for parents; it meant the loss of valuable and costly therapy time—time that had already been paid for. Rescheduling or make-up sessions were not an option, so we all shared in the responsibility of maintaining good health for our kids and ourselves.

This was an ongoing challenge, considering the less-than-desirable level of hygiene practiced at the center at that time. Children drooled and sneezed on mats, tables, trays, balls, and toys used in the course of therapy. Equipment appeared well maintained and safe, but I never noticed it being wiped down or sterilized between patients. Sheets and drapes were not always changed, either. Hands were not washed. Most parents, us included, carried bottles of hand sanitizer and wipes to wash hands following each session throughout the day. Like most Americans, we were obsessed with sanitation, at least in the beginning. Later, we relaxed when we realized we weren't going to change anything while we were there and that we might as well go with the flow. And none of us ever got sick.

Aimee had very limited speech at this point, although she could say a few simple words. She said them often and sometimes repeated them over and over. We knew she wanted to talk. Her physical abilities were extremely limited and she could not sit, crawl, or stand independently. When placed on the floor, she lay flat because she had no arm or leg strength to raise herself up—like an infant who hasn't yet begun to crawl. Individual therapy programs were established for each child based on his or her abilities and on the preliminary medical examinations conducted by staff physicians.

The physical therapists made it clear that the success of the therapy would largely depend on Aimee's ability to understand instruction and her willingness to do the work. She received therapy at home, but certainly not as complex or intense. She often did not cooperate with her home therapists, and we wondered if she would cooperate now, especially since she didn't understand a word they were saying—even with a translator. Although similar in some ways to her home therapy, the length and frequency of each session was greater. It was clear to us that the children were expected to focus and cooperate. We bought into this concept and clearly understood that much depended on Aimee; however, we had serious doubts about whether she was up to the task.

Euromed's methodology included an intensive twenty-eight-day regimen designed to meet the specific needs of each child. Teams of therapists worked with the patients over a six-hour day, six days a week. Aimee had three therapists: Kristina, the team leader; Edwina, the resident therapist; and another Kristina, an intern. Her program began at 7:45 a.m. when warm gel packs were used to relax her joints. This was followed by massage and Adeli suit therapy for two hours. Then from 10:00 a.m. to 10:30 a.m. another therapist administered positioning therapy. Resistive weights and pulleys were used to strengthen muscles and reinforce the correct pattern of movement, or positioning, of each limb while the patient remained in that position for thirty minutes at a time. Next was movement therapy followed by a half hour in the stander. And that was just the morning.

After a much-deserved thirty-minute break, a therapist named Violeta introduced the Spider, a device prescribed for Aimee, that concluded the routine for the day. The "spider" therapy prescribed for Aimee involved exercises focusing on the legs while she was being supported with a wide belt connected to bungee-type cords attached to a room-sized frame. Deep knee bends, standing up straight, bearing weight, squats, leg stretches, and a variety of other exercises were all rewarded with "flying" on the spider at the end of the session. After she got used to it, Aimee laughed and squealed with delight when she was able to fly. This was not the case, though, in the beginning.

Lunch was served in the cafeteria between 1:00 p.m. and 2:30 p.m. Optional art and music therapies were available in the afternoon. We missed most of the optional classes because Aimee was exhausted and took a long nap almost every day.

Therapy didn't start smoothly. The first day was directed toward orientation only—meeting the therapists and discussing the therapy program developed for Aimee. On the second day, when therapy actually began, Aimee cried for forty-five minutes, increasing in intensity, until she was gagging, choking, and gasping for air. As we progressed through the various therapy stations, this scenario was repeated over and over, resulting in Aimee's absolute exhaustion—not to mention our own.

Allowed in the room on the condition that we remain silent, Janise and I watched with aching hearts as Aimee screamed in terror. We fought to control our own tears and clutched each other's hands, not knowing what to do. Silent looks at each other confirmed our shared concern: Should we stop the therapy or sit tight? I was as concerned about Janise as I was about Aimee. It was clear that Aimee wasn't being harmed in any way, or in pain—as far as we could tell—but she screamed at the top of her lungs as if she were being tortured. Perhaps in her own mind she was. So far, all they had done was to put her in the suit. This was not a painful process and was as simple as getting dressed, but it was obviously frightening to Aimee. The therapists just continued to reassure her with patience, hugs, and soothing words in Polish. Nothing they tried would calm her. She wanted absolutely no part of them, or their therapy, and was communicating that in no uncertain terms.

Finally, the suit came off and Aimee immediately calmed down. Within minutes, she was smiling and making her "kissing" gesture to the therapists as if nothing had happened. Saying "bye-bye," she couldn't wait to get out of the gym and, frankly, neither could we. The most amazing part was seeing Aimee's manipulative behavior in action. We were astonished at her determination not to cooperate with anyone in any way.

Aimee kept smiling until we entered the next therapy room for positioning, which must have looked like a torture chamber to Aimee, judging from the change in her expression. She was positioned on the table and with the use of pulleys, weights, and arm braces was placed into a "crawl" position. She screamed at the top of her lungs. No amount of reassurance from the therapist or us would calm her down. She did not know what was happening to her or why, even though we tried to explain. We endured another thirty minutes of hysteria as we watched Aimee fight back with every bit of physical and emotional strength she could muster. Aimee could not crawl, nor could she support her body weight with her arms and knees. The purpose of this exercise was to develop and familiarize her body and brain with the idea of crawling. But for her, bent into a position that was completely unfamiliar, she clearly felt entirely out of control. It *was* terrifying, not only to Aimee but to us as well, even though we understood the logic behind it.

At last we had a break in the schedule and time for a snack. Janise did not feel well and went to see the staff doctor. I was concerned and knew she couldn't tolerate much more stress. At her request, I agreed to take Aimee by myself to the next therapy session.

The final session of the day was the spider, consisting of simple weight-bearing exercises to develop and build muscle strength. I was certain Aimee would cooperate, but I was wrong. She cried even more, becoming stiff and rigid as she carried on. I attempted to console her but all she said was, "No, no, no, no, no!" The therapist, beautiful Violeta, ignored her cries and tried to solicit Aimee's attention, but she refused to cooperate. At last, the session was finished. I breathed a sigh of relief and returned Aimee to our room, where Janise was resting quietly.

If it had not been for the encouragement of other parents, I have no doubt we would have packed up and left for home that day. But we decided to heed the advice of so many others, who assured us that after a day or two her terror would end. Aimee would be fine, they said. We would see. We knew we couldn't quit now. We had traveled so far, and saved and raised enough money for the therapy. Going home now meant we would be giving up on Aimee and limiting her opportunity for improvement. We knew we had to be strong. We knew this was our only chance and agreed we would stick with it at all costs.

So we came up with a plan. I would take Aimee for the start of each session in the morning. This would protect Janise from having to endure Aimee's screaming and clinging when she was handed over to the therapists. Janise would join me after the therapy started and, we hoped, after Aimee had calmed down. It was a good plan and we were comfortable with our strategy—so much so that after lunch, we returned to our room and fell asleep until dinnertime.

Aimee's resilience astounded us. Just hours after her hysteria, she was happy to see the other children and extended her hands. She wanted to touch and relate to the other kids. She ate heartily, without complaint, and was her usual happy self, as if nothing had happened out of the ordinary that day. Tomorrow was a new day. We prayed we all would do better.

. . .

Following breakfast, I took Aimee to her first therapy session. Kristina, the lead therapist, wanted to make a deal; she communicated the new plan through our interpreter, Irina. She would allow us in the gym to observe Aimee during the last half hour of the session only. Our presence was distracting, and Kristina felt Aimee would focus better if she were not compromised by our presence. Wanting to cooperate, I reluctantly agreed, knowing that, in reality, she could simply ask us to leave.

I sat in the busy hallway on a low, narrow bench and tried to read while listening to Aimee scream and cry. It was extremely stressful. After all, Aimee was only three, and I worried she couldn't fully understand why we had abandoned her. When Janise arrived I explained the situation. She joined me on the bench where we sat together every morning for the next four weeks.

Aimee cried for the first fifteen minutes and then stopped. We heard laughing. We heard crying again, then quiet. Then, once again, laughing. We peeked into the room through a crack in the door, without Aimee seeing us. She was exercising in her Adeli suit and smiling. We were flabbergasted to see Aimee bonding with the therapists and communicating with them—in spite of the fact that they didn't speak or understand English and Aimee barely spoke at all.

Finally, we were allowed in the room and observed Aimee standing upright in the suit and, with the aid of the therapists, actually taking steps forward. We couldn't believe our eyes! Ecstatic to see us, Aimee headed in our direction, clearly proud of herself and her accomplishment. It was a fantastic moment. We were overjoyed with her newfound attitude.

With the same strategy in place, I took Aimee to the positioning therapy next. Only this time she and I had a little talk first. Our agreement was that if she didn't cry, she could listen to music, which was agreeable to the therapist, but if she cried, the music would be turned off. Aimee couldn't talk, but I knew she understood the consequences if she cried. I had done this before and she knew I would stop the music if necessary. She especially liked to listen to Elmo and responded with smiles at my suggestion. Although she remained somewhat defiant and fought the positioning, she managed to control her tears when reminded and was rewarded by listening to her music. This helped tremendously. It became our routine throughout the remainder of the month. Music was allowed only during positioning therapy. The calming effect of listening to music she enjoyed not only helped Aimee focus but also occupied an otherwise boring time for her. This was an opportunity for me to teach her about music—instruments and rhythm—as we listened together. Janise and I traded off sitting in the room with her and keeping her entertained. Aimee wasn't perfect, but the hysterics were behind us.

After our break, I took Aimee to the spider, where she did better and did not cry at all. She was beginning to accept the routine and saw the other four children in the gym doing the same thing. It was also reassuring for me to watch other children with their therapists. I observed each child's desire to please. Aside from occasional tears, all were engaged and happy to be there. The exercise was difficult and often appeared painful, but Aimee managed to tolerate the unfamiliar body movements and get through the sessions. We rarely heard anyone cry. It gave us confidence in ourselves and courage that we—and Aimee—could make it through to the end.

. . .

Each day got better as Aimee made progress. Some days were hard, when the therapy involved positions or movements that Aimee could typically not perform; even so, she managed. Janise and I waited outside the gym every day. I worried that the stress of therapy might provoke a seizure, something Aimee never had, and wanted to stay close if anything unforeseen happened—and for that reason one of us always remained close during the therapy sessions.

A week had passed when Janise suggested we switch roles—she wanted to be the one to take Aimee to her sessions, which meant I would join her outside in the hall after each therapy session began. I had no objection, except that I didn't think we should change our routine, because it was working. Aimee was adjusting nicely to the program. Her mood was cheerful and positive when I took her and left her with the therapists, but when Janise was present, she would whine and cry for her mother, which took time and attention away from a positive start. That's why the therapists did not want us in the room in the first place—it kept Aimee from focusing and listening to *only* their instruction. Aimee is a creature of habit and thrives on routine and consistency. She was comfortable with the therapists and even liked them but challenged them when in pain. Returning for the second week of therapy had been difficult for her, especially after having Sunday off.

On this particular Monday, she cried in the Adeli suit and was irritable and tired. Janise insisted on taking her to the spider therapy alone, where Aimee cried and screamed. Finally, Violeta concluded the session early because Aimee refused to listen. Janise was equally frustrated when she returned to the room. We had a strong difference of opinion as we discussed the situation. I decided that I needed some time to myself and went for a long walk. Janise needed time alone too and took a nap with Aimee.

I spent a quiet afternoon in Koszalin. On the way back, I rode the bus with the local commuters and returned to Mielno that evening after dark. I had dinner alone at a local restaurant followed by a walk back to the center. It was good for us to have some time to ourselves. I needed it. We both needed it. The stress had gotten to both of us. Janise wanted to be more involved, and as long as it didn't disrupt Aimee, I agreed and encouraged her to do so. I was too overprotective of her pregnancy and needed to grant her the freedom to determine her own limitations. After all, she was an adult. She needed to permit me to do things my own way too.

When I returned to our room that evening we were able to have a calm and meaningful conversation and map out a new plan for the remaining three weeks. It was an important moment in our relationship, then and now. Foremost in our hearts was our mutual goal to help Aimee succeed. I had made a commitment to Janise that I would stand by her in this endeavor no matter how difficult it became.

But it wasn't easy. Janise and I were homesick and irritable. Janise had never traveled out of the United States before. After talking, we laughed at ourselves and confided that we had both been unreasonable and difficult. Time together in Poland under such duress gave us an opportunity to build a strong and trusting relationship. To this day, Janise encourages me to participate in all of Aimee's medical appointments and school conferences. It is a privilege I appreciate and one I feel I have earned. My resolve and commitment to help Janise with Aimee remains unfaltering. We had made this long journey together for Aimee's benefit. The time had come to count on each other to make the best of the situation.

• • •

Through this experience and others we have learned that Aimee does not do well when her mother takes her for any unfamiliar, or sometimes even familiar, activity. Perhaps it is insecurity, desire for attention, the closeness she feels to her mother, or simply fear. Whatever it is, Aimee often refuses to cooperate with Janise. This includes doctor visits, X-rays, haircuts, and a variety of other activities. Typically, in anticipation of this behavior, Janise will ask me to intervene and accompany Aimee. Janise does not baby Aimee in these situations; Aimee simply does not do what is asked of her and becomes extremely difficult for her mother to manage. I've seen it happen time and time again.

One ongoing example is Aimee's refusal to sleep in her own bed at home. Janise has called me and said, "Listen to Aimee. She doesn't want to go to bed!" I listen in disbelief to Aimee, who sounds as if she is being tortured. Nothing quiets her. I have a great deal of respect for the patience and tolerance my daughter-in-law exhibits in these situations. I'm grateful Aimee has never done this to me when she sleeps at our house or travels with us.

• • •

Aimee continued to do better as each day passed. One evening, midway through the course of therapy, Aimee stunned us: She began speaking in sentences. Three sentences to be exact, all appropriate in sequence and content. I had been reading in bed, in the dark, with a little book light turned on low. "Grammy, put out the light!" Aimee said. Then, "Grammy, go to sleep!" And again, "Put out the light!" Janise and I couldn't believe our ears! This was an immense, and unexpected, accomplishment for Aimee, and we were thrilled beyond words. Her speech improved considerably as she began saying new words, memorizing songs, and counting aloud.

This event was only the beginning for Aimee, whose speech began to blossom. Not only did she say, "good morning" to the therapists in Polish but also to other children in their respective languages— Italian, Polish, and English. It was amazing to us that she knew and remembered each child by name. Even though she didn't see well, she knew who they were by their voices or some other means. She referred to the men in our group as "grandpa" regardless of their names or ages. We praised and encouraged her to keep talking—and she hasn't stopped since.

• • •

Living at the center involved many daily tasks and chores. We shared housekeeping responsibilities and made every effort to maintain order in our tiny room. Only Aimee fondly referred to it as "home." Janise did the wash and survived the laundry room from hell. Imagine the implications of fifty families sharing three washing machines and one dryer during the month of January in Poland! An ongoing saga of will and strategy unfolded as women raced for control of the equipment. Washers were in constant demand from 7:00 a.m. until 10:00 p.m. when the laundry room door was locked. To add to the insanity, the staff also used the equipment to wash linens for the entire facility. This usually happened during the night but sometimes carried over into daytime hours. It was a truly bizarre situation and one that evidently continues to this day. We managed to survive by hanging our clothes on the radiator in our bathroom to dry, which was inconvenient but better than the alternative.

Patients were given room and dining room table assignments, apparently based on family size, country of origin, and seniority. Americans were housed on one floor, and Europeans and people from other countries on another. The same was true of the dining room, where Americans ate with Americans at assigned tables, Italians with Italians, Germans with Germans, and so on. Even so, when time permitted, we all socialized with one another whenever possible. Three meals a day were served at regular intervals. We were not required to eat in the dining room, but we were required to pay for all meals provided during our stay whether or not we ate them.

Aimee, unlike many of the other children, liked the food and ate heartily. Delicious chicken soup, prepared in every variety imaginable, was served daily as the first course for lunch. That was followed by a main course of chicken, fish, or pork with mashed or fried potatoes. The meals were tasty, nutritious, and well prepared. But many of the American kids were picky eaters and ate very little; some ate only food that was shipped from home. We had shipped very little food other than a couple of cans of tuna and just ate what was served. We even expanded our taste for Polish food. One of Aimee's favorites was the delicious roasted chicken sold only at little roadside kiosks in Koszalin. Another was afternoon tea, which we enjoyed every day at 4:00 p.m. along with cookies or fruit. Aimee fondly referred to it as "hot tea, tea hot time."

• • •

We quickly became acquainted with other families. There were twin girls from Boston who were five years old and similar to Aimee and Chloe. Only one of the twins had cerebral palsy, the other was fine. There was another pregnant woman from New York City with her son; he had microcephaly like Aimee and didn't walk or talk. Interestingly, there were two other sets of twins at the center during our time there. One was a set of teenage boys from Italy and the other a set of girls from Poland. Each had one disabled twin and one normal twin. This was important for Janise, who learned that she wasn't alone in having twins in this situation. In fact, according to the therapists, it was not uncommon at all.

Approximately twenty-five American families were there, four of us for the first time. Most of the other families had been there at least twice. We soon realized this was a remarkable place. The advice and encouragement from seasoned parents proved invaluable in making our stay a positive experience, especially for Janise.

We managed to go out several times for dinner as a group, especially when a couple of the dads were willing to help with the wheelchairs. It was dark by 5:00 p.m., and no one ventured out without warm clothing, an umbrella, and a flashlight. Regardless of the subzero temperature, everyone walked together to and from the restaurant, a multitude of flashlights lighting our way. The kids were bundled up in snow gear, hats, mittens, and blankets to protect them from the cold.

With special-needs kids, this was not a simple, routine task. Getting the children in and out of their wheelchairs just to remove jackets took time and was difficult. Regular chairs in the restaurant had to be removed to accommodate the many wheelchairs around the table. Selecting menu items further complicated the already chaotic process.

Restaurant staff did not speak English and only partially understood what was ordered. We Americans did not speak Polish, except for a few words. Food items were prepared differently than assumed from the menu description. This produced tears of frustration and disappointment for the children when the meal was delivered to the table and it was not what they wanted.

Food eaten, children sleepy, and adults refreshed with an evening out, we went through the entire process again in reverse for the walk home. The real treat, of course, was the camaraderie shared by all in enjoying an adventure together. Being so far from home without familiar friends and family was lonesome and boring. But sharing experiences, concerns, and accomplishments of our children with our newfound friends—all in the same boat—intensified the overall pleasure of being together. Sunday brought the sleepy village to life. Local grandparents, parents, and children walked the promenade, and even the beach, as they flocked to restaurants and cafés enjoying family time together. It was amazing to see couples, often seniors bundled in fur coats and heavy jackets, walking arm-in-arm on the beach, the ice crackling in the sand under their boots. Everyone seemed to have a dog.

But Sundays were especially difficult for me. I missed my own family at home, even the dog, and longed to be with them. I have no doubt everyone else felt the same. Janise and I made every attempt to keep Sundays special. We would go for long walks together, go out to lunch or dinner, or maybe hire a driver to take us to another village to enjoy the afternoon. It was our only day to enjoy leisurely outings, if the weather permitted.

Then, one Sunday, at the end of the first two weeks, the facility arranged a day trip for the group to Gdansk, approximately three hours away by bus. Gdansk, a beautiful and charming Old World city, is located in the northeast region of Poland. It was a wonderful outing, although unbearably cold, and just what we needed to get us through the final two weeks of the session. By this time, lasting friendships had developed, and we enjoyed sharing activities with other families.

• • •

Janise and I established and adhered to our daily routine as the month slipped away. Every day was the same: Janise fed Aimee breakfast and I took her to therapy; I fed her lunch, then she and Janise took a nap. I took a long walk each afternoon and enjoyed the quiet time to myself to reflect on the day. Later, I would write in my journal and prepare tea for us. But things had changed. Aimee's behavior was outstanding. We marveled at how her attitude had improved and how well she adjusted to all aspects of our new environment. We could not have asked her to be better than she was. We were truly proud of her!

In addition, she began to open her hands, uncurl her toes, and gain upper body control. She walked with assistance in the Adeli suit and enthusiastically participated and cooperated with her therapists. In fact, to our surprise, she became quite fond of them and was eager to see them every morning. She sang songs, recited sentences, and repeated simple nursery rhymes and poems. We were unbelievably pleased.

One night, while Janise was in the shower something remarkable happened. I waited patiently until I heard the water turn off and called to Janise to come quietly and look at Aimee. She did and was astonished at what she saw. Aimee had been sitting up, cross-legged, by herself, for almost twenty minutes! She was still doing that when Janise entered the room. I handed Janise my video camera and she documented this special achievement. We were both in tears, amazed at her strength and ability to balance herself on her own. Aimee managed to hold herself in this position several more times that evening before falling over. I will never forget the joy of that moment and what a special gift I had been given on my birthday.

I tried to teach Aimee to sing "Happy Birthday" to me in the days preceding my birthday. She never liked the song and definitely didn't like the clapping she knew would come at the end. Startled, she would cry as soon as she heard "Happy Birthday" and no amount of encouragement would get her to sing it. Finally, the day after my birthday, she began singing the words, "happy birthday to you!" repeatedly throughout the day, to me and to herself. It was a day late, but not too late at all.

• • •

Pleased with the results, we soon began to speculate about the possibility of a return trip. Of course, it was Jason and Janise's decision, not mine. After talking with Janise about it, I knew that, if it happened, I, alone, would be the one to bring Aimee. Janise said she would not entrust Aimee to anyone else to travel such a long way. Now that she had experienced the therapy for herself and was familiar with the routine, she felt she could send Aimee with me, and I was confident I could do it. Of course, there was still the question of cost. I planned to talk with Mel when I returned home about financing a second trip.

Saying good-bye to everyone in Poland was bittersweet. We had made good friends. We had learned about each other and ourselves. We had met the challenges head-on during this extraordinary experience, and we rejoiced in the accomplishments of these children who had all worked so hard. We were sad to part ways, but the time had come to pack up and prepare for the long journey home.

• • •

Our entire family was at the airport when we arrived in San Francisco: Mel, Jason, Chloe, Janna, and her husband, Greg. I had missed them, my friends, and other relatives. Mel and I maintained a very social lifestyle, and I yearned to chat with friends and plan an evening out. I also was looking forward to time with my husband, and he surprised me by planning a weekend at the coast. Long walks on the beach, dinner at our favorite Carmel restaurant, and quiet time together to catch up on all the news was just what I needed.

I had no doubt that Janise felt the same. She was tired and, now over six months pregnant, physically uncomfortable. She just wanted to get home. It had been a long month and at last we were reunited with our families, safe and sound. Aimee was excited too. She understood that we had returned home and couldn't wait to see her Daddy and her "Sissy," as she referred to Chloe.

It had been a remarkable journey for all three of us, one we would never forget and that could never be duplicated. At times it felt like we were on an emotional roller coaster, but we survived the ride. Janise and I were proud of our accomplishments, but that was miniscule in comparison to how proud we were of Aimee's. Our lovely little Aimee had enlightened us with her abilities and overwhelmed us with her determination to succeed. She entertained us with her humor and blessed us with her affection. It all happened because we took a risk— and Aimee embraced the opportunity and didn't let us down.

TERROR STRIKES

MY SON WAS NOT HAPPY WITH ME. We were at odds about the benefits of returning to Poland for another therapy session. He reluctantly supported the first trip but didn't expect us to come back wanting to go again. He agreed that the first trip was successful and helped Aimee tremendously, especially with her speech. "But," he asked, "was it really necessary to go again?" How many trips did we plan to make? Certainly we didn't plan to do this every year, did we? How were we planning to pay for it? Who would take Aimee there? He was adamant that Janise not leave Chloe or the new baby, once it arrived, at home again. Our debate became a cold war between us that went on for months.

Of course, we both knew the final decision was his to make, not mine. I was the grandparent—not the parent. But I couldn't help myself. Defiant, I persisted. Helping Aimee was my goal. Recognizing her ability to improve and her determination to do so, I felt she deserved every opportunity to reach her potential. I didn't intend to see her fall short, even if it meant challenging my son.

While in Poland, we had talked with the physicians about Aimee's progress and the benefits, if any, more therapy might provide. They could not say that she would ever walk or even crawl, but there still were many gains to be made that could improve her overall quality of life. Our hope starting out was that she would walk. In truth, we would be thrilled to see any improvement. She did talk, which was an absolute blessing in itself. Aimee's ability to talk and communicate is truly a remarkable gift and one that was completely unexpected. Additionally, muscle development, bearing weight, maintaining upper body strength, achieving head control or the use of her hands, and sitting straight in her chair were all wonderful goals—any number of which could be accomplished.

Janise and I made two decisions before leaving Poland. The first was to leave a deposit and reserve a space for the next available session, which was in August 2001. The second was to purchase a special-needs stroller before leaving Poland that I could use on a return trip with Aimee. This would minimize the need to travel with her wheelchair, making it less cumbersome for me in the event we returned alone. Both decisions and investments proved to be worthwhile. I was already laying out the logistics of a second trip in my mind. The challenge would be to convince my son.

My husband bought into the idea of another therapy session in Poland. He, too, felt it would beneficial for Aimee's continued development and improvement. To my surprise, he reminded me that I was a seasoned, experienced traveler and even encouraged me to make the trip alone with Aimee. She behaved well when she was with me and had traveled well on the first trip. There was no reason we couldn't do it.

We also discussed financial options and agreed that we could fund the second trip. To me, it was obvious that Aimee had been challenged and stimulated by the experience, developing confidence and maturing as a result. Whether it was because of the actual therapy or the one-on-one attention, she blossomed in the months that followed. I knew I could not deny her the chance to go again.

Jason, on the other hand, didn't agree and felt it was too far away and too long a trip. He lined up his supporters and I lined up mine. I knew I was pushing the limit but held my own. His biggest supporter, in my eyes, was his father, my ex-husband Jim. He felt it was ludicrous to make a second trip and saw no benefit to Aimee whatsoever, claiming that we were imagining the improvements. "Aimee is what she is," he said. "Why are you trying to make her something different?"

When the kids were in town, we often had dinner together, including my ex-husband and his wife. Our evenings usually ended with a debate about whether putting Aimee "through this" really made a difference. This went on for months, without being resolved, but we would have to make a decision soon.

• • •

Janise had a beautiful baby boy, Jeffrey, in May of that year. Understandably, much of Jason's anxiety lifted when Jeffrey was born in perfect health. Responsible and concerned about the baby's well-being, Jason withheld his final decision about Aimee's therapy until after Jeffrey was born. Janise pleaded with me not to give up on taking Aimee, but I was growing weary of challenging my son and didn't want to compromise our otherwise positive relationship. But I also supported Janise and was compelled to help Aimee.

Finally, when I was almost out of time to make the necessary plans, Jason said yes, making it clear he would not allow anyone but me to take his precious child halfway around the world. I appreciated his confidence and assured him I would protect Aimee with my life. I didn't know it then, but my words would echo in his ears many times over.

I booked our tickets and used my accumulated miles to upgrade to business class. This would make our journey more comfortable and make it easier for me to manage with Aimee alone. We planned to meet Harvey and his twelve-year-old son, Matthew, who had made the trip to Euromed many times, in London and fly to Berlin together. He had arranged for a private driver to take us across the German border into Poland and on to Mielno. Harvey was pleased that we would share some of the travel expenses. I was relieved that we would not have to fly into Warsaw as we had done before. I looked forward to this alternative route, and meeting Harvey for the last portion of our trip would be an immense relief to me.

Aimee and I settled comfortably into our seats on the plane. When the attendant asked where we were going, I explained. To my surprise, Aimee, who was listening to our conversation, told her, "Some day I'm walking!" Our flight to Chicago was uneventful and when we arrived an airline employee assisted us to the international terminal, which greatly reduced my stress.

We arrived in London on time, but our prearranged assistance never did. I had been told that a van would meet us when we landed and that we were not to take the regular airport shuttle to the terminal. As directed, we remained on the plane and waited. Two shuttle buses came and left with the other passengers. When no one arrived for us, we were escorted by a flight attendant off the plane to the bottom of the stairs and told to wait on the tarmac. The attendant assured me that someone would "show." The flight crew then left. Another twenty minutes went by and no one came.

Fortunately, another van arrived to pick up a small group of male passengers traveling to Israel. They were required to go through security at a special terminal location and were being transported there. As they boarded their van and prepared to leave, I began to panic. We would be totally alone once they left, so I asked the driver if he could help us. Reluctantly, he agreed to take us to the "handicapped assistance" desk, where they would certainly be able to help.

Aimee and I were loaded into the van and driven off through the bowels of the airport. I had no idea where we were or where we were going in relation to our departure gate. I tried to remain calm so that I could focus on what I needed to do next. After fifteen minutes of driving under the terminal buildings, he exited into daylight and pulled up to the curb and pointed to a door. He told me to enter there and that someone would assist us. He helped us out of the van and sped off.

When we reached the door, it was locked! I pushed and pulled but it would not open. The man sitting at the desk inside rudely waved me off. I knocked and knocked, but that only annoyed him more and he ignored me. I continued to knock and each time he waved his arms, indicating I should leave. Persistent and frantic, I continued knocking until he angrily marched to the door and through the glass shouted, "This entrance is for disabled assistance only. You must go to another terminal!" I tried to explain through the door that Aimee was handicapped, but he refused to listen. Finally, in desperation, I grabbed the disability tag that Mel had attached to Aimee's stroller and pointed to it. When he saw it, he responded in shock and immediately unlocked the door, apologizing profusely. Aimee's stroller had thrown him. Familiar with handicapped adults in wheelchairs, he had only rarely seen a child in a wheelchair and never one in an adaptive stroller, so didn't recognize Aimee's disability.

Time was running out—we had just twenty minutes before our flight left the departure gate. He looked at our tickets, grabbed my bags, and shouted, "Follow me; we must hurry if you are to make your flight!" We literally ran through the airport, up and down elevators, through doors and hidden hallways, and finally emerged inside the passenger boarding gates. Our airplane had been fully boarded. Remaining at the gate until the last moment to board were Harvey and Matthew. Harvey was certain we must have missed our connecting flight and they had waited as long as possible for us. It was a close call. I took a deep breath and smiled at Aimee's delight when she heard their voices and instantly recognized "Grandpa" and Matthew.

In Berlin, Harvey's driver met us and our troubles were over. We were in good hands and only had a few more hours to go. The driver, Christian, a kind and gentle man, greeted us with a big smile and went into action immediately, strapping the children in their seats and retrieving our luggage. We were on our way within minutes.

Aimee had once again been an excellent traveler: no tears, no complaints, and no problems—an angel all the way. I was relieved when we arrived safely at Euromed. Now familiar with the routine, we quickly settled in. Euromed was packed with families. It was mid-August and the weather was beautiful. Most parents do not want their children to miss school, so the summer session is the most popular. There is usually a long waiting list for this session, so I considered us lucky to have reserved a slot. There was, however, a compromise.

Our room was even tinier than the first one had been, and it was at the end of a dark hallway with the only window facing a noisy street. It had only one twin bed and one small futon-type bed. There were no closets and only two small shelves for storage. Our clothes were stacked in plastic containers and our personal supplies, along with empty suitcases, were stowed under the bed. A blow-up pool toy creatively served as Aimee's bathtub and we were lucky it fit, barely, on the bathroom floor. But we had a room. I wondered how in the world we would manage when Mel arrived for the last week.

• • •

The weeks passed quickly and Aimee was wonderful. She surpassed my expectations in her behavior, her attitude, and her determination. She was joyous at seeing her old friends and the therapists she had come to love. She didn't cry for her parents. She didn't cry during the physical exams and evaluations. In fact, she didn't cry at all, not even during therapy. Her only moment of anxiety took place when we went to an outdoor party. Everything was fine until the birthday cake arrived! Once the group began to sing "Happy Birthday," it was all over for Aimee. She wanted to leave. Aimee's fourth birthday was a week away, on August 21. I had planned a little birthday party for her but now decided against it. Instead, I invited Harvey and Matthew to join us for dinner at the local Meduza's Restaurant, Aimee's favorite, on the beach in Mielno. Aimee was thrilled. I requested that no one sing "Happy Birthday."

The summer months are very hot in Poland. And, as is traditional throughout Europe, everyone goes on holiday during August. Poland is no exception and Mielno, a popular destination with Germans and East European tourists, was bursting at the seams. Every previously empty lot or parcel of land was covered with travel trailers and tents. The sidewalks were packed, the restaurants were full, and the beach was covered with sunbathers. The ice cream kiosks and snack bars were bursting with long lines of people waiting to be served.

There was a food booth for everything imaginable and it was all delicious. Aimee and I sampled everything at least once. This was completely different from being there in the dead of winter. Every evening, we went out for a long walk in the village or along the lakeshore. It was wonderful. I will never forget the village as it was that August. The lake across the main boulevard was surrounded by carnival rides, souvenir booths, and food stands. The entire village was alive and bustling with activity.

It all came to an abrupt end on September 1. Within days, the entire village was empty. Kiosks were closed and locked, food stands disappeared, tents were folded up, and trailers were hauled away. The show was over and summer had ended. The tourists headed home and Mielno returned to the sleepy little village I had known previously. By the time Mel arrived in early September, almost everything was closed.

Mel arrived to spend the last week with us and help with our return trip home. He was especially interested in Aimee's daily workouts. He intently observed every aspect of her therapy and actively participated when permitted. Her routine was exactly the same as before, with the same therapists. Aimee thrived and worked hard, but no matter how much she tried, she still could not crawl or walk. They said she needed more work to strengthen her arms. Even then, no one was sure how much it would or could help. Nevertheless, Aimee did well. She had more torso control, was bearing weight, and could even stand independently while propped against the bed. I took a photo of her smiling while standing in this position. She was so proud of herself!

Aimee won the hearts of her therapists and they fondly called her "Movkra," little ant, in Polish. Her chatty personality, positive attitude, bright eyes, and big smile kept everyone entertained. She can be quite funny, likes to tease, and enjoys interacting with other children and adults. Watching her and the other children, their affection for each other obvious as they reached for each other's hands, would often bring me to tears.

The dedicated therapists are remarkable. They are kind and loving, yet they do not tolerate any lack of attention or cooperation from the children. Even with a language barrier, their expectations are made clear and the children comprehend and work hard to achieve their goals. In the course of a month it was easy for them to become very attached to their patients, each unique and a gift in his or her own special way. Some kids cannot talk, some cannot walk, but they all have an innocent and loving quality in common that cannot be explained. It is something you feel when you are with them—a type of affection and unexplained energy. This is how it is with Aimee.

During the session, Aimee worked extremely hard to crawl but she couldn't—her arms were not strong enough to support her torso. Unfortunately, her spastic extension and involuntary movement kept her from bending her knees. Still, she continued to try and often said, "Grammy, some day I'm walking!" Her expression of this dream always brought a lump to my throat. What could I say other than to encourage her to keep trying? I thought it was unfair to say it was not possible; yet, I wondered whether it was unfair to allow her to have a dream she might never realistically be able to achieve.

• • •

It was the afternoon of September 11, 2001, and we were packing up in preparation of our departure the next day. The last session was in the morning, and Christian would be picking us up after lunch on September 12. We planned to spend a night in Berlin, fly to London with Harvey and Matthew, and then begin our journey back to California.

It was about 3:00 p.m. when I took Aimee down the hall, where she was invited to have tea with her little friend Annie. I chatted for a moment with Annie's mother and then walked back to our room, where Mel was watching a soccer match on a German television network. The door was open and as I entered the room, the TV was showing an airplane crashing into a very tall building. They were speaking German and I couldn't understand what they were saying. Then, a caption came across the bottom of the screen in English saying that an airplane had hit the World Trade Center in New York City. Was it true or fiction? We watched in horror as they played the tape over and over. Mel tried another station but the best he could get was BBC. Then the second airplane hit and we knew it was real. I ran down the hall to tell the other Americans to turn on their televisions. They did so and everyone became silent with shock. Soon the sound of weeping and lamenting was heard coming from the rooms up and down the hall, and we gathered in the corridor to console each other.

One of the parents worked for a New York electrical firm that was assigned to do work on the towers that day. He was distraught with worry and fear for his fellow workers. None of us could access telephone lines to call home. Finally, after several hours, my children were able to reach us by phone, relieved to talk to us but worried about our safety in getting home.

We discussed our options. All the airplanes in the States had been grounded. We had no idea how or when we were going home or what we were going to do next. The interpreters at Euromed told us there would be a special meeting for the American families that evening at 6:00 p.m. to discuss departure options. The administration informed us that we were safe at the center and could remain there, free of charge, as long as necessary until alternative arrangements were made to return home. We had a long private conversation with Harvey, since we had planned to leave and fly to London together. Harvey's wife worked for an American airline carrier, and she called as often as possible to give him current updates of the situation. BBC was the only English-speaking television network available to us, but it provided news only from England and not the States. For hours the news was speculative and unclear. Harvey told us, as was later confirmed, that the London airport was filling up with over 20,000 stranded travelers. We were also informed by several reliable sources that there were no hotel rooms available and that all flights to the United States were canceled. We realized that even if we could get to London, there were no accommodations for us there. Traveling with Aimee in her stroller and Matthew in his wheelchair complicated and limited our options.

There were so many questions left unanswered. What if we got to London and couldn't leave? Where would we stay? Where would we go? It was maddening. The airport staff in Berlin recommended that we remain in Berlin because all flights out of London were canceled indefinitely. The airline representative in the States, however, recommended that we try to get to London and be there for our scheduled flight to Chicago on September 14. We were assured that if they were flying again, and we had tickets in hand, we would likely get on that flight. But, if we missed that flight for any reason, we would have to wait a minimum of ten days to get another flight out of Europe. No one had all the answers.

We still had hotel reservations in Berlin and decided to call Christian to pick us up. Anticipating our situation, he was already on his way. Fortunately, he correctly assumed that we would want to leave Poland as soon as possible. We were grateful for his insight and thoughtfulness. We arrived in Berlin and drove directly to the airport to confirm the status of our flights out of Berlin the following morning. Our tickets remained valid and our flight had not been canceled. Departure had also not been confirmed. We kept our options open.

Christian remained with the children while we talked to the airline representatives. We were still uncertain about what we should do but decided we would go to our separate hotels and reconnect later that evening. We exchanged telephone numbers and said our good-byes to Harvey and Matthew in case we didn't talk with them in the morning. Our decision became clearer when Harvey called later that evening to tell us that he and Matthew were leaving for London in the morning and from there he planned to fly to Canada, where he would rent a car and drive them to their home in Utah. Initially, we were thinking we would stay in Berlin. Because of the circumstances, our hotel agreed to provide us with a room as long as we needed it. This was fortunate for us, considering that hotel rooms were at a premium in Europe.

Aimee was our primary consideration. We knew that Jason and Janise were concerned but understood that we would probably not communicate with them again until we were back in the States. They assured us that they had every confidence in us to make the best decision possible and would stand by until they heard from us again. Awake and unable to sleep, Mel and I discussed our situation into the early morning hours. We decided that we would take our chances: Our flight to London had not been canceled and we planned to be on that flight in the morning. We weren't sure what would happen after that.

We packed our bags and called Harvey, who said he would instruct Christian to pick us up in the morning on the way to the airport so that we could leave Berlin as originally planned. The hotel staff were extremely concerned for our safety when we checked out. It was a relief to learn that they would hold our hotel room for two days in case we had no alternative other than returning to Berlin. Comforted by this generous and caring gesture, we knew we had a place to stay if all else failed.

Aimee was visibly exhausted. She didn't understand what was happening but instinctively knew something was wrong and repeatedly asked if we were okay. Our flight to London was uneventful, but we were completely dismayed when we disembarked. The airport was packed with thousands and thousands of people crowding into every corner. We somehow managed to collect our bags and drag them to the curb. Desperate to get to the international terminal, we flagged down an "out of service" bus to help us. To our surprise the bus actually stopped. I'm certain that the driver recognized our desperation. And then there was Aimee. Two Middle Eastern men helped us to get Aimee and our bags on the bus. We learned that flights were leaving. If that was accurate, we had just thirty minutes to make our plane.

We had no idea where the international terminal was in relation to where we were. We put our trust in the bus driver. Finally, the bus came to a stop about one block from the terminal. This was as close he could get. It was impossible to see the entrance doors to the building because people were lined up as far as the eye could see.

I grabbed our carry-on bags and hung as much as I could on the back of Aimee's stroller. Mel took a cart he found on the bus and piled on the luggage. I yelled for him to follow me, sure that somehow I would get us inside. He couldn't imagine how I would accomplish it but followed me without question, nevertheless.

I believe that God gives you strength to handle the unexpected. This was one of those situations. Tickets in hand, I was determined to get us in that terminal—no matter how many people were waiting in line. I had no intention of going to the end of the line, either! I walked right up to a security guard with an American Airlines patch on his jacket and begged his help. I explained that Aimee was disabled and didn't walk and that I was her grandmother. I showed him our tickets and told him our flight was scheduled to leave in twenty minutes. We needed to make that flight or we had nowhere to go. He looked down at Aimee and looked back at me. Mel was still walking toward us as fast as he could with the cart full of luggage.

"Yes, madam, you need to get inside!" he said. "Stay right here and I'll get you help." Thank God! He called on his radio and within minutes a woman was at the door to escort us inside. With only a nod, she grabbed the tickets out of my hand, looked at them, took hold of Aimee's stroller, and started pushing her way through the crowd. Her only words were, "Follow me and stay close."

The crowd was huge and dense. People were literally standing shoulder to shoulder. She parted the crowd as she pushed ahead. The barrier of bodies closed behind her before I could keep up. Mel struggled as well. He tried to stay close on my heels and keep both of us in sight. I grabbed the back of the woman's jacket and held tight. With the other hand I grabbed on to a suitcase behind me on the cart. Somehow, I don't know how, we managed to get to the ticket counter. I was extremely concerned about Aimee. She had been pushed, bumped, and banged getting from the door to the check-in counter. I didn't hear her cry; in fact, I didn't hear a sound from her at all. When I was finally able to check on her she had a big smile on her face and said, "Hi, Grammy, I love you!" I leaned over and hugged her and praised her for being such a good girl. She was fantastic and I knew we were going to be okay.

I looked up from Aimee and glanced around the terminal. I was deeply saddened at what I saw. At that moment, I realized the seriousness of what had occurred. I have never witnessed a crowd of people in such a state of desperation and anxiety. People were pushing and crowding each other everywhere I looked. Hundreds of individuals were pressed tightly side by side as they slept on countertops and the floor. Every available surface was covered with people desperate to get home.

I assumed the woman who led us through the crowd was a supervisor or manager of sorts. To us she was an angel. When we arrived at the counter she threw up her arms and waved her hands in the air. In a loud voice, almost shouting, she said, "Everyone, listen to me now! These people are next in line and I don't care who has been waiting, they are a priority!" As soon as the first transaction in the system finished, she jumped in front of that window and called for me to follow.

Once again she threw up her arms and said to the counter staff, "I want everyone to stop what they're doing right now! I need these seats back and they're off the computer!" With authority she announced, "No one can issue seats until we find them." It was a critical moment. Our tickets had been released from the system; if they were gone now we would have lost them within minutes of our arrival at the airport. After all our efforts, this just couldn't happen. Everyone stopped. We waited.

Finally, an attendant shouted, "I found them! They're still here!" What a relief!

Our tickets were reissued to us. It had been a very close call. Mel, only a few feet behind me couldn't hear what was going on but was anxiously waiting to know what was happening. We were informed that, although it was delayed, the flight was scheduled to depart and would be the first American Airlines flight leaving London for the United States. We knew we were fortunate to be on it.

Next, the woman said, "Take everything out of your purse except your wallet, your tickets, and your passports." She continued with her instructions, "Put everything you have in your bags. Hurry! You cannot take anything with you on the plane except your purse." That was it; no carry-on bags, no camera, nothing! Understandably, security was extremely tight. Mel didn't want to give up his carry-on bag, or the new video camera with which he had lovingly documented Aimee's therapy. It didn't matter, she said; all of it had to go into a plastic bag. She tied the top of the bag and put a tag on it. Away it went on the belt with the other items. Aimee was allowed one diaper only. No snacks, no water, and no toys. We had nothing with us except the clothes we were wearing and my small purse. Fortunately, Aimee was allowed to remain in her stroller and even that had been carefully scrutinized.

Once again, the woman pushed through the crowd, and we followed as she led us to a primary security area. After going through security with us, she instructed us to wait there until another manager arrived to take us to the next security checkpoint. Then she said good-bye and wished us a safe trip home. Soon, another woman came and escorted us to a second security area. This process took an hour. By then we were exhausted, hungry, and thirsty. We were assured there would be some refreshments at the gate. But when we finally arrived at the gate, the only refreshment available was bottled water.

It was now almost 4:00 p.m., and Aimee hadn't eaten anything since breakfast. She told me she was hungry but I had nothing to give her, not even a mint! There was nothing to buy. There was no food in sight anywhere! We took our water and were grateful to have that. It was another hour before we were finally given permission to board. We were required to go through still another security check at the boarding door. It was frightening. At last we were on the plane and felt relieved and happy to be there. We were more scared than we had imagined we would be. Everyone was tense and suspicious.

Safely buckled in her seat, Aimee turned to me and said, "Oh Grammy, I'm so hungry." For the first time in my life, and only for a brief moment, I experienced the helplessness one must feel when there is no food for one's child to eat. We were hungry, but far from starving, and we knew food would be available soon. I could only imagine how terrible it would be to live with this fear daily.

I asked the steward if there was anything Aimee could eat. He said, no, not until after the plane took off. Now, practically begging, I implored him to find something, a little snack, anything that would satisfy her hunger. He returned with a little bag of crackers. It was all he had, but it was enough. I fed them to Aimee one at a time. She ate them with gusto and promptly fell into a deep sleep. She didn't wake until we landed in Chicago, and for that I was grateful.

In Chicago, Mel took over. I stayed with Aimee while he managed to get us on a flight to San Francisco. I was finally able to call Jason and Janise. I told them we were safe, in Chicago, and would be home some time the following day. Their fears were alleviated when they knew how and where we had landed. They just wanted us to get home safe.

There were long waits between flights, and there were few, if any, options for a flight to the West Coast. We were grateful to be on any flight as long as it would return us home. Coincidentally, the attendant at the airline desk in Chicago was Polish. As we approached the counter Aimee cheerily said *"Gendobre"* to her in Polish. "Good day," she responded. Then she asked where we had been and Mel explained that we had been in Poland at Euromed.

"Your original tickets were first class to San Francisco," she said. "I'm going to give you first-class seats on this plane, too, so you can sit together. You deserve it after everything you've been through." Exhausted, we very much appreciated the luxury seats.

At last we landed. I broke down and cried when we hit the runway. "Thank God we're home!" I said to Mel. It was past midnight when we arrived at our house and we went directly to bed. Jason and Janise arrived the next afternoon to pick up Aimee, and she was excited to see them. We shared our stories of the last few days. Jason and Janise told us that as long as Aimee was in our care, they knew we would keep her safe.

SOCIAL EXPECTATIONS

"**AFTER ALL THIS,** I'm sure this is the last time you'll be going to Poland," said Jason. "We'll see," I said with a smile. He didn't know I had already placed Aimee's name on the waiting list for January, only four months away. This time it was going to be a very tough sell, but I would do my best to make it happen.

Things settled down in the weeks following our return. Aimee started school and did well. She was the only child in her class of ten special-needs children who talked. And talk she did, especially with adults. She kept her teacher and aides entertained with her funny comments and stories.

Aimee still believed that some day she would be able to walk. She said this often. I thought that perhaps she was feeling empowered by the therapy. After all, being placed in the Adeli suit allowed her to move her body in different ways. In particular, it gave her the feeling of standing upright and crawling even though she could not do so on her own.

She also received therapy at home. Although not as intense, it clearly helped her maintain what she had gained at Euromed. Working the muscles and developing strength and coordination definitely helped Aimee sit up straight in her chair. She could hold her head erect without being harnessed. The therapy also helped her keep her hands open, although her arms remained tight and held close to her chest. Her speech improved further. Her listening skills had also improved, as she was now expected to follow instructions even though she often acted silly and laughed when she was expected to perform a task.

Aimee blossomed when she started school. Always social, her ability to speak clearly allowed her the means to express herself. This often meant talking nonsense to anyone who would listen! Of course, coming from a family of talkers, this was no surprise to us. Sometimes Aimee would openly express her feelings. "I'm sad," she would say. Or she would demand acknowledgment of her presence when she was ignored. She would say, "Come over here," or "Talk to me." Her favorite way to get someone's attention is always to comment, "I want to ask you something." Aimee's strong desire to be recognized and included has kept her in the spotlight. Never a wallflower, her strong personality and character are endearing to all who meet her. But her talking, even now, often gets her in trouble at school. Instead of listening, she interrupts. Instead of answering questions, she repeats them back. She often becomes silly when she should be serious.

Kindergarten was familiar to Aimee because she continued in the same classroom with the same teachers as her preschool. She loved her teachers, especially a man named Daniel who was clearly her favorite. She expressed how much she "loved" him to anyone who asked her about school. "I love Daniel," she'd say. I visited Modesto often and went to Aimee's school to observe her in class. Aimee would burst with pride and excitement when I arrived. "It's my Grammy!" she'd exclaim loudly as soon as she heard me speak, even if it wasn't to her.

And, if I deliberately didn't speak, she would listen intently, knowing that someone had entered the room. I wear lots of bangle bracelets and always the same perfume. I am certain these are traits that Aimee knows well and that help her recognize me when I am near.

As the school year progressed, Aimee began to say, "Daniel loves Sandy." Sandy was the director of the department and apparently

Daniel's boss. There was never any indication or evidence that Daniel and Sandy were romantic; in fact, quite the contrary—Daniel was all business with Sandy. So no one thought much about it when she began to mention Daniel and Sandy. We just smiled and knew she liked them both. She began to talk about them at home, and she talked about them when she visited us. One day I asked Janise, "What's the deal with Daniel and Sandy? Aimee keeps saying, 'Daniel loves Sandy' and then laughs." Janise explained that Aimee said the same thing at home and that it was simply nonsense because Aimee liked talking about school. Daniel and Sandy gave her something to talk about and talk she did. We laughed it off.

Just before the end of the school year, Daniel and Sandy dropped a bombshell when they announced they were recently married. We were even more shocked when they announced that Sandy was pregnant. Aimee's astute perception was right on. When I visited Aimee's school, I congratulated the parents-to-be and mentioned Aimee's comments. They laughed and replied that Aimee often told them the same at school, even though they had never, under any circumstances, given any indication that they were in a relationship. Even their coworkers didn't suspect. Aimee's keen intuition and sense about people would exhibit itself many times in the future. So often, in fact, that we began to listen more intently when she spoke.

Aimee did well at school but still had one big problem when it came to participating in the weekly assembly. She screamed in fear when wheeled into the auditorium with other children. She absolutely could not tolerate clapping or the microphone. It was similar to her fear of "Happy Birthday," because she anticipated the clapping at the end of the song.

Janise invited me to attend Aimee's Individual Education Plan (IEP) meeting at school along with her and the school principal, Aimee's teacher, the regional caseworker, speech therapist, physical therapist, and occupational therapist. In these meetings Aimee's progress and goals are discussed. The topic of Aimee's fears was discussed. I made a commitment to myself to work with Aimee to help alleviate her anxiety and fear and to broaden her tolerance of noisy settings and public places.

Jason and Janise avoided taking Aimee to restaurants, pizza parlors, game centers, and noisy places as much as possible, because she would cry and become so uncomfortable that it compromised the activity for everyone. When she did go with the family, she was expected to behave along with her siblings. Mel and I enjoy eating out and have always taken Aimee to restaurants with us. She enjoys this, perhaps because she has our undivided attention, and has learned from me that she must maintain certain restaurant manners. When dining out in a restaurant, she must say "please" and "thank you" and must not chew with her mouth open or spit out food. When she is full she says, "I'm finished," so that I know when to stop feeding her. When she says it, I honor it and conclude her meal.

Feeding Aimee is a notable process. First, she cannot chew certain foods like lettuce or raw leafy greens. They are difficult for her to swallow because they are flat and without texture. Food pieces must not be too large so that she can chew and swallow them without difficulty. Sometimes Aimee gags, but she rarely spits out food. If she gags, I stop feeding her. It means she is either full or dislikes the taste. When introducing new foods, which I often do, I remain on alert just in case. She also makes her own menu selection from the items offered. I typically take two items from the children's menu and tell Aimee what they are. She decides what she wants and orders it for herself. I've encouraged this independence but limit it to two selections to avoid confusion and overstimulation. If there are too many choices, she cannot focus or make a decision. Overall, Aimee has impeccable manners and enjoys all types of food.

Directions, reassurances, and expectations must be explained to Aimee in a detailed but concise manner. Patience is key to her understanding. And this is exactly how we solved the "Happy Birthday" problem in restaurants, which had become so debilitating for Aimee that I felt it should be our first priority. First, we started by consciously avoiding sitting next to any large group that might be there to celebrate something. We turned Aimee's chair and positioned her so that she faced away from the patrons in the restaurant, especially if it was crowded. If I saw waiters heading toward a table carrying a cake with candles, I immediately started talking to Aimee about something silly or funny to distract her. Sometimes this worked and sometimes it didn't. Aimee knew that she wasn't allowed to scream or be too loud in a restaurant. Her father would absolutely not allow it. So, little by little, we tried to get her more comfortable in this setting. As simple as it may seem to the average family, this was a big issue for Aimee and for those helping her cope with her anxiety.

I tried to anticipate restaurant problems before they happened so that our evening wouldn't be ruined. Aimee would ask me, "Who's talking so loud?" or "Who is that laughing like that?" Sometimes she would be curious about another table and ask, "What are they doing over there?" I began to realize that she, too, was evaluating her surroundings and whether anyone was "having a party." I acknowledged these individuals by saying to her, "Aimee, they are here to celebrate, just like us." I explained that people liked being together to share special occasions and that was why they sang "Happy Birthday." I also encouraged her to sing and clap her hands, which I helped her to do. Gradually her anxiety began to lessen. I was happy to report this progress at her next school meeting. Her instructors had also noticed an improvement at school assemblies.

I believe this method worked because, when quietly speaking with Aimee one-on-one, she can listen and comprehend. If, on the other hand, there are too many noises or too many voices talking at once, she cannot concentrate and does not understand what was said.

• • •

As part of our Christmas tradition and celebration, I had taken Chloe to *The Nutcracker* ballet twice and had not included Aimee for obvious reasons. We assumed that Aimee would be incapable of tolerating the dark theater, the microphone, and the applause. So Chloe and I went alone. On the third year, Mel went to Modesto to pick up Chloe and bring her to San Jose to attend the ballet and spend the weekend. Aimee was excited to see him, and when she saw him exclaimed, "Tutu, guess what? I'm going to *The Nutcracker* with Grammy today!" Mel was confused since he thought he was only picking up Chloe, not both girls. Aimee was obstinate. She was certain she was going too.

Perplexed, Mel immediately phoned me to ask if he had misunderstood. I gasped in surprise and told him that I didn't buy Aimee a ticket and, in fact, didn't even consider doing so. I had believed she wouldn't be able to tolerate it. I was upset and felt terribly guilty. I felt as if I had betrayed Aimee by not including her in our plans and perhaps I had. I decided then and there that I would never make that mistake again. I would include her next year.

RETURN TO POLAND

CHAPTER 10

THE HOLIDAY SEASON was quickly over and we were preparing to leave for our third trip to Poland on January 28, 2002. Jason had agreed this time but hoped it would be our last trip to Europe. "Isn't there another program here that you can take Aimee to?" he asked. "No, unfortunately there is not," I responded, but I agreed to research other options when we returned. Euromed had expressed interest in opening a center in the States but nothing had materialized yet.

Aimee, now four, and I made the trip to Mielno alone. We were completely on our own this time and travel had become considerably more complicated. Our flight itinerary was San Francisco to Cincinnati, then Cincinnati to New York, New York to Paris, and finally Paris to Berlin. In Berlin we would meet our driver, Christian, who would take us to Mielno and Euromed. Aimee had a little cold in the weeks preceding our departure.

When we left, she did not have a fever and appeared to be better. I was confident she would be fine. She was excited about the trip and happy but seemed lethargic and slept most of the way from San Francisco to Cincinnati. By the time we left New York, she was not feeling well. She didn't want to eat or drink. When our attendant offered ice cream, though, Aimee perked up and we ordered a sundae. Mistake! She happily ate it all and soon she began to complain that she felt "sick" and wanted me to hold her, which I did. Then, without warning, she threw up all over my sweater, herself, and the seat.

The attendant quickly appeared and came to my aid with a handful of napkins and paper towels. Everything was a mess and smelled. I quickly changed Aimee into another set of clothes, not an easy task on the plane while she was strapped to her seat. My favorite black cashmere sweater was soaked in vomit. Unfortunately, due to the limited carry-on space, I had neglected to bring a change of clothing for myself. I had nothing to wear except my wet bra and a jacket that had one button at the waist. I didn't even have an extra T-shirt with me. I took off the sweater, rolled it into a plastic bag, wiped off my bra with a damp napkin, and wrapped myself in a blanket for the remainder of the flight. It was quite embarrassing.

I was stressing over what I would wear when we got off the plane when, just before landing, I was approached by an unfamiliar attendant. She had heard about my dilemma from another employee and offered an idea. She wore a "cut-up" T-shirt under her suit to keep warm on the plane. She would be happy to give it to me so I would have something to wear under my jacket. I thought it was pretty funny, but I was desperate. The T-shirt had been cut very low in the front and the sleeves had been removed exposing uneven, unfinished edges. It was better than nothing and I was grateful that I didn't have to wear only a bra and I could get off the plane without being indecently exposed.

We had a three-hour layover in Paris and I had time to buy a new T-shirt. Aimee became feverish and continued to gag and vomit. I assumed she had the flu but couldn't do much about it then. We found a quiet lounge area where we remained until it was time to go. I laid her down, gave her some Tylenol, and tried to force fluids. She refused to eat. I requested medical assistance at the airline counter, but there were no doctors or nurses in that section of the airport. Our flight to Berlin was short, but Aimee's condition remained a concern. Christian, our reliable and trusted driver, was waiting when we arrived. He took over and soon we were on our way to Mielno, where I could contact a doctor for Aimee.

By the time we arrived, Aimee was ill and very dehydrated. I was extremely worried about her. A physician was on call and knocked on our door within minutes of our arrival. She examined Aimee, who by now had a temperature of 102 degrees. The doctor instructed the interpreter to go to the pharmacy for medication, liquid vitamin C, and an atomizer. Along with the treatment, she ordered some chicken soup for Aimee, who ate a little of it and quickly fell into a deep sleep. Evaluations were scheduled in the morning, and I feared Aimee would not be well enough to start therapy the day after.

To my astonishment though, Aimee was better in the morning. We made it to her physical evaluations and she slept most of the day. By the following morning she was completely recovered. Smiling and well, she was able to start her therapy as scheduled. I was impressed with her care and relieved that she was better.

Aimee essentially had the same routine as previous sessions—the same therapists and therapy. She enjoyed being there and continued to work hard. Every evening after dinner at Aimee's request, we "walked the hall" as she called it, so we could visit with others on our floor. This was followed by a warm bath, a massage, and a bedtime story. As always, Aimee's behavior was excellent. She never cried, ate well, and delighted in time spent with the other children at the center.

• • •

One morning, Aimee wanted waffles. I had never eaten a waffle in Poland or seen one on a menu. I decided I would surprise Aimee by making waffles in our room. I needed a waffle iron but had no idea where to buy it. I had purchased a hair dryer, curling iron, and VCR on previous trips and certainly should be able to locate a waffle iron now. I checked with other parents and the hardware store in the village but had no luck. Finally, on a mission to locate and buy one, I drew a picture for our interpreter. She finally understood what I wanted and arranged for a taxi driver to take me to the appropriate store in

Koszalin. In addition, she prepared a grocery list, in Polish, of the ingredients that I needed. Polish markets in that area did not have waffle or pancake mix, so I had to work with the basics.

On Sunday morning when we could sleep in and relax, I delighted Aimee with waffles for breakfast. She smacked her lips as she ate. Eating waffles in our room on Sunday mornings became a cherished tradition for the remainder of our stay.

• • •

Mel arrived during the last week of the session and would accompany us home. The month had been a success in that Aimee had gained significantly more muscle strength. I didn't know when or if we would return but decided to leave a deposit for the August 2002 session. We were placed on a waiting list.

We concluded therapy a day early and planned to spend some time in Berlin before returning home. It would give us all a chance to relax and recuperate. Aimee was tired but, as always, enthusiastic and willing to do whatever we planned. On the morning of our departure, as advised, we arrived at the airport early. Security had tightened and we needed to plan our time accordingly. To our surprise, and by coincidence only, several other families from Euromed were on the same flight to Paris.

• • •

When booking flights, I always inform the airline that I am traveling with my granddaughter and that she is a disabled child requiring travel with her wheelchair. Sometimes we used the stroller instead, but whether wheelchair or stroller, it remained Aimee's means of mobility and had to be taken with us into the cabin. We were scheduled to fly on a foreign airline, although I had booked our tickets through an American carrier.

When we approached the desk to check in, we were notified that we would have to wait for our boarding passes until a physician arrived at the airport. "What physician?" I asked. We were informed, along with the other parents, that our children would not be allowed to board until they were seen by a physician who would evaluate each child.

At that time, the physician would review the required "medical documentation" certifying that our children were capable of air travel. I wondered to myself how they thought we got there in the first place! None of us had any such "certificate" in our possession. We were outraged and felt it was an unrealistic demand on the part of the airline. We argued to no avail and were told it was the policy of the airline now being enforced, apparently because there were too many of us for a single flight. The official told us that only two children and their families would be allowed to board.

The physician would determine who that would be, out of the eight handicapped children waiting for the plane. Unfortunately, the rest of us would have to reschedule our flights, they said. We also were told that the European airline carriers were not required to comply with our ADA regulations.

We were all placed in one room, where we waited. Finally, we were told that the physician evaluation would be waived. Each parent would be required to sign a document releasing the airline of responsibility. Furthermore, we had to check strollers and wheelchairs *before* boarding the airplane, and they would be returned to us in Paris. Keep in mind that most, if not all, of these children required their wheelchairs for mobility; without them, they would have to be carried. Reluctantly, we all complied and checked the chairs as required. Last, that same representative told us that if any crisis occurred on the plane we had to remain seated with our children until all other passengers had disembarked first. Finally, four hours behind schedule, the plane departed for Paris. Many people on our flight missed their connections in Paris and had to make alternative arrangements.

Unfortunately, this situation brought to light the reality of traveling with disabled children and adults overseas. The ADA, which Americans take for granted, prohibits such discrimination. In a foreign country, we were at the mercy of their laws and how those laws were interpreted by the person in charge. In this case, it had been an inconsiderate manager who took it upon herself to enforce discretionary guidelines. This inappropriate decision was equally thoughtless and inconvenient for the many business travelers and other passengers who were on the same flight. It was a lesson I would not easily forget for future travel with Aimee.

• • •

In Paris, we had difficulty rescheduling our flight home. Unbelievably, the wheelchairs and strollers never arrived—they were lost. Consequently, people had to carry their children. Mel managed Aimee. I was grateful he was with us because I could not possibly have carried Aimee and our bags if I had been alone. When Mel could no longer hold her, he sat on the floor with her while I argued with the ticket agent.

We had used our accumulated air miles to upgrade our tickets to business class. It is the only way I can efficiently manage Aimee and her needs in the aircraft. We had lost that status on the alternative flight the airline offered, not to mention that we were being routed to four different flights to reach San Francisco.

I vehemently refused to accept this alternative plan. Finally, after much heated discussion, we were offered business class seats with another carrier. There was only one problem: The plane was preparing for departure as we spoke. To make the flight, we had to rush to a gate located in another terminal. At my insistence, the woman reluctantly stood up from her desk and accompanied us there. Mel had to carry Aimee and I had to manage our bags. Without her guidance we would have never found the remote desk and would have missed that flight, too.

Our stroller was finally located and returned to us two weeks later. Travel can be an ordeal and traumatic under the best of circumstances. I learned that you must always be prepared to deal with situations out of your control. Traveling with children increases the risk that something may go wrong—but traveling with a disabled child with special needs makes the entire process even more challenging.

THAT'S AMORE, THAT'S LOVE

CHAPTER 11

WHILE IN POLAND, I listened to dozens of parents talk about their creative fund-raising efforts so that they could continue to bring their children for therapy. The Adeli suit program is rarely a covered or reimbursed medical expense. Parents had the desire to provide the therapy for their children but often lacked the financial ability to do so, at least on an ongoing basis. Unless they had a large medical settlement or independent funds, it was hard to afford Euromed therapy or, for that matter, any other special therapy. I thought there should be a better way to help these children and their families.

At that time, total expenses including travel and therapy were approximately $12,000 to $15,000 per trip. We came up with our own creative fund-raising: I was inspired by Janise's uncle Grant and a group of Modesto businessmen who knew about Aimee and her therapy trips to Poland and organized a fund-raising dinner for Aimee in 2001. Experienced with community volunteerism, they quickly organized a group and implored their friends to participate. The idea escalated from a restaurant dinner for fifty to an outdoor barbeque for more than two hundred guests. Their event was a success and their generosity helped make it possible for Aimee to attend another therapy session. Mel and I continued to cover the travel expenses.

I knew from our own experience that people who met Aimee instantly wanted to become connected and involved. I call it the "Aimee phenomenon." It happens often, even with strangers. Such an occasion unexpectedly happened when my brother gave a cash gift for Aimee's therapy. On another, we were invited to visit distant relatives. They had met Aimee once before when they visited us in San Jose and asked us to bring Aimee to their home so their grandson could meet her. Their boy, a little older than Aimee, spent the entire afternoon with her and had as much fun pushing her everywhere in her chair as she had riding in it. They had a wonderful time together and we enjoyed watching them.

After we said our good-byes and were ready to drive off, they handed Aimee an envelope and asked that we not open it until we were on our way. Reluctantly, I agreed. After prying the envelope from Aimee's tight grip I opened it. A heartfelt and beautifully written note was enclosed along with a cash gift of $1,000 toward Aimee's therapy. What a surprise! It was a sincere gesture on behalf of their entire family to help Aimee, one we will never forget.

These events inspired me to create a nonprofit foundation for children with special needs. Many families needed help to afford continuing therapy, and this would be a way to assist them. Hiring a consultant to set up the foundation was too expensive. I decided I would find out how to do it myself. Having no experience in this area, I went to my accountant for advice. The application process was lengthy and complicated. It took weeks to complete and required a name, a mission statement, and a board of directors. Additional requirements included operational guidelines for administration, fund-raising, distribution, and accounting. There were pages and pages of questions requiring careful consideration and comprehensive answers.

I decided to call it That's Amore Charitable Foundation, Inc. The motive behind the name was Aimee's favorite song. She was passionate about Dean Martin's rendition of "That's Amore" and enthusiastically sang along with every word. She listened to it over and over and literally wore out several recordings in the process. It was the perfect name, I thought: *amore*—love. What could be more inspiring than a little girl who is loved by all and who has so much love to give in return?

Our mission statement was direct: "To increase public awareness through fund-raising activities sponsored by That's Amore Charitable Foundation, Inc. and to develop the full potential of children with special needs."

Establishing a board of directors was a little more complex. I used the resources of family and friends to put together a professional board consisting of business people, health professionals, and community volunteers. Once completed, the application was submitted. After several months of waiting, we received notice that we were officially a nonprofit foundation. I was delighted. In the future we would help numerous children and their families realize their dream of having a better quality of life through therapy. And we could help Aimee.

• • •

During our most recent therapy session at Euromed, parents began talking about several similar therapy centers opening in the United States. These were not affiliated with Euromed but were independents that were offering similar therapies. One of these centers was located in Southern California. I was eager to find out more.

Mel and I traveled to Los Angeles on business several times a year. On one such occasion, we decided to visit the new center located in Anaheim. I was impressed. Although small in comparison to Euromed, the facility, the therapy, and the program were almost identical to that offered in Poland. With the exception of one American therapist, the therapy staff were all trained in Poland. I immediately recognized two therapists I had met in Mielno. I later learned that the owner of the center had been to Poland with her son on several occasions and was inspired to open a center of her own.

After thoroughly evaluating the new center and talking to parents who had been there, I approached Jason and Janise about taking Aimee there. Janise still preferred the Polish program. Jason, however, was pleased at the prospect of remaining close to home. They could visit and, more important, he could observe Aimee's therapy for himself. The overall cost, considering accommodations and meals, was equivalent to making the trip to Poland, but I could drive us there. Another plus was that I could easily remain in touch with home. I reserved a slot for the June 2002 session. We would be there for four weeks, and I made arrangements to stay at a local Residence Inn located close to Disneyland and shopping and entertainment venues. We would have plenty to do for the month and Mel agreed to visit on weekends. I looked forward to making the trip with Aimee when school was out. Jason and Janise also planned a short vacation in Southern California. It was a perfect plan. My daughter Janna and my sister Diane also planned to visit. For once, everyone was happy.

• • •

Aimee continued to improve. She was talking more and doing well in her special-needs class at school. She was cognizant of her surroundings and engaged in interacting with others. By now, taking Aimee to therapy had become routine for me. We enjoyed each other's company, and when I took her for the month, it gave her parents a much-needed break.

Aimee requires assistance 24/7 for her existence and is totally dependent on others for her hygiene, feeding, dressing, and educational and entertainment needs. This is her way of life, and it requires the nonstop attention of her caregiver. As much as her parents missed her, they welcomed the break. It was also true that with Aimee away, the other children could enjoy time with their parents and the routine activities of family life, which were otherwise taken up with caring for Aimee.

Because of her limitations, Aimee is easily bored, so keeping her entertained can be a challenge. At that time she could not hold a crayon or pencil to color or draw. She wanted to color and that could only be accomplished with assistance. She would tightly grip the crayon, often breaking it, and then hold her arm rigid so that she couldn't reach the paper or move her hand once she did. Sometimes the "feel" of the crayon on the paper bothered her and she resisted moving it at all. Puzzles, games, and toys requiring fine motor skills were usually too difficult for her to manage.

Aimee doesn't see well and can watch television or a movie only if she is very close. I believe she watches movies by *listening* rather than watching. She can hear very well and enjoys auditory activities—such as listening to music, reading books, and playing word games—the best. She participates in reading by turning the pages by herself, especially once she has memorized the book, as she often does.

Aimee is a sponge for learning. Without a doubt, entertaining and teaching Aimee is a challenge requiring much patience, but the joys and rewards of doing so prevail over any hardship related to her care.

• • •

In June 2002, the same group of Modesto businessmen hosted a second fund-raising dinner event for Aimee. It was another success, and they decided to make it an annual event. A large barn in the country equipped with a kitchen, restrooms, and even a space for dancing was the perfect venue for this summer's hoedown. Aimee and I left the morning after the fund-raiser for Anaheim.

My Suburban was packed to capacity. The drive took approximately eight hours from Modesto, during which time we listened to music and stopped along the way for breaks and lunch. Aimee understood where we were going and eagerly anticipated making the trip. We arrived at our hotel and checked in. The SUV unpacked, we settled in our small but efficient space. Dinner out was reserved for the weekends, when Mel could join us. There was no cafeteria or restaurant at the hotel, so I prepared lunch and dinner in our suite. Complimentary breakfast was served and simplified the morning rush to get to therapy on time.

Aimee was a little apprehensive the first day of therapy but quickly bonded with her therapists, two young women from Poland. Perhaps she sensed my initial anxiety. In Anaheim, there were no physicians on the premises to perform a medical evaluation prior to therapy; that responsibility was left to the therapist. I brought Aimee's hip X-rays, expecting an orthopedic specialist to look at them, but there was no such physician on staff. This gave me cause for concern, especially after I had signed the required release form as Aimee's guardian.

During these trips, I have a notarized letter from Jason and Janise with me at all times, authorizing me to make medical decisions for Aimee. When applicable, Jason and Janise provide me with a similar letter, authorizing me to take her out of the state or country. I am well informed regarding Aimee's medical status and feel confident that I would make a wise decision if I needed to. On this first trip, I scrutinized the facility carefully and watched the therapists with a keen eye until I was satisfied that everything was safe.

The facility consisted of one large gym and several small therapy rooms. There were ten children enrolled for the month. Five would attend morning sessions beginning at 8:00 a.m. and five would attend afternoon sessions beginning at 1:00 p.m. Most of the children were from California, but some were from other states, including the East Coast. Most of the children ranged in age from four to twelve years of age. I was completely surprised to see even a toddler receiving therapy.

The suit and positioning therapist worked with one assistant and did both therapies consecutively. A separate therapist did the spider therapy, which was somewhat different from what we had experienced in the past, although it appeared very effective. Aimee's sessions were from 8:00 a.m. to 12:30 p.m. daily, five days a week, with two breaks. There was no therapy on the weekends. This was nice for a change, but I thought that most parents would have preferred six-day-a-week therapy.

A tree painted on the lobby wall with stick-on appliqués had the names of those children who had attended the facility. I recognized many of the names from Poland and, in fact, knew three of the families that were there with us at that first session. The new center seemed to operate efficiently, and Aimee and I quickly fell into our routine. I remained at the center with her every day, often observing and assisting when necessary. I regularly took a short walk to the neighborhood market for coffee or snacks.

In Poland, Janise and I had been impressed with the skill and knowledge of the therapists. They were focused, dedicated, and disciplined and expected the children to appropriately respond and participate in therapy. In Anaheim, the Polish therapists were excellent but lacked the strict discipline enforced in Poland. The environment here was much more relaxed, and the owner of the facility was off-site. The responsibility was on the parents to observe and supervise their own child's therapy and progress, a role I gladly accepted.

Aimee did well and the results of the therapy were positive. The summation by her therapists at the end of this session was essentially the same as the conclusion of the Polish physicians: Aimee had very limited strength and little function of her arms. This made it impossible for her to crawl. Without crawling, she could not walk. It was a concept I understood only too well. They recommended that Aimee wear arm braces daily. I had purchased expensive arm braces in Poland for this purpose and had given them to Janise. I explained the reasoning behind it and that Aimee should wear them daily. The muscles in her arms had to be stretched in order to relax. They could not be strengthened if they were constantly flexed, which prevented her from bearing weight on her arms. In the therapy suit, with arm braces, Aimee was able to crawl with assistance, but she could not do so independently. Even so, Janise disagreed that the arm braces would help and did not use them, feeling that they were confining and difficult for Aimee to wear.

• • •

Jason and Janise visited Anaheim during our stay. Aimee was elated when her father spent the day with her at the center. Sometimes he observed from outside the room—out of her field of vision. Aimee constantly asked, "Is my Daddy watching me?" "Is he watching me now?" "Where's my Daddy?" Her well-deserved praise from him resulted in very big smiles.

I noticed my son observing the other children, too. I sensed his level of emotion as he looked away. It was that familiar sorrow and heartache one feels when touched by these children. It is not pity for them but admiration for them and for their parents, who love them so much. Regardless of the level of disability, hope never dies. The lump in your throat comes when you see that reflected in the eyes and hearts of everyone there. They are all doing whatever they can to improve the lives of their children.

• • •

My husband arrived for the weekend the day before Jason and his family left. One of Mel's traditions since the girls were born is to buy their Halloween costumes. "Tutu" delighted in making it an annual event, and that year was no exception. Aimee and I had already been to the Disney Store on several occasions and she wanted a costume. I explained to her that we had to wait for Mel and her family to come and then we would shop together. She knew she wanted to be a "princess" and she talked about it constantly. Her age-appropriate behavior in this situation amused me and, although annoying, warmed my heart. She understood the concept of Halloween and anticipated wearing a special costume. She also recalled countless activities associated with the holiday.

We met at the Disney Store that afternoon. Chloe and Jeffrey picked out their costumes and accessories to match relatively fast. They knew what they wanted and went for it. Aimee was more complicated. Disney has a variety of princess characters and we had to look at them all— over and over. We walked around and around the display cases, an exercise I had already done several times before.

Janise and I held up one costume after another as we offered sugges- tions and encouragement about each one. "No, no, no, no, no!" Aimee would say. "No, not *that* one; *that* one!" This continued forever, as she insisted she would pick her costume soon. We took costumes off the racks and held them close to her face so she could see. She looked carefully, her head turning side to side, and then she said, "No!" We showed her shoes, crowns, wands, and accessories; she wasn't interested. She wanted to pick a dress first.

She looked more and then, finally, made her decision. "I want to be *that* princess," she said. She continued, "You know, *that* one. I want to be Cinderella. I want the blue dress!"

Aimee had managed to command our attention for over an hour and enjoyed every moment of doing so. I cherish that recollection and remember how it made my heart swell to watch this determined little girl—who could control so little in her life—take charge of making her own decision, on her own terms. We enjoyed dinner together and then returned to our hotel with Aimee. Jason, Janise, and the kids returned to Disneyland for the evening and left early the next morning for home.

We had one week of therapy remaining, and Janna would visit next. Janna had followed Aimee's progress from the beginning. Because Aimee's therapy was now in California, she had an opportunity to visit the center and observe Aimee in action. "Emotional" would be an understatement to describe Janna's reaction. The children drew her in and touched her deeply. She held their hands and talked with them all, even those who could not respond verbally. When Janna saw Aimee in the therapy suit going through her exercises, tears filled her eyes and she had to walk away. She was amazed by Aimee's exhibition of vigor and strength and her ability to comprehend instructions. She could visit only a day and was sad to leave so soon, but I promised her she could return again the next time we came to Anaheim.

THE PEACEMAKER

CHAPTER 12

THE THERAPY IN ANAHEIM was less intense, but Aimee benefited nevertheless. And it had been a productive month. She was thin and frail when we started but had developed muscle and gained weight at the end. Although the therapy met Aimee's needs, we felt it was less effective than the program in Poland. Jason didn't buy it and we had to compromise—Anaheim would do just fine. I was pleased that this was an acceptable solution for everyone, and it was certainly better than no therapy at all. I reserved a slot for Aimee at the Anaheim center for the January session in 2003.

The physical results of therapy often take weeks to materialize. The psychological gains from the therapy were apparent at once. Aimee's poise and self-confidence grew. She talked nonstop with the therapists, even those who weren't working with her, and knew them all by name. She said "good morning" to everyone and often knew who arrived by the sound of their car. She remembered who ate what for snack and which child had which therapist. If someone cried in another room she told me who it was and why they were crying or, in some cases, laughing. The therapy seemed to heighten her perception of life around her.

• • •

Aimee possesses a magical ability to relate to others, and because she is always a delight to have around, she is included in many invitations from our friends. Our best friends, Myriam and Mario Cordero, are a lively and colorful couple from South America. Doctor Cordero was there when the twins were born. Being the loving friends that they are, they have demonstrated unconditional support and encouragement and have always been interested in Aimee's progress. Aimee has loved them from the beginning. They often entertain Aimee when "Tio Mario" plays the piano and "Tia Myriam" sings—not unlike the popular Charro! Aimee delighted in their attention and could never get enough of them. In return, she has charmed them when she sings along with them in Spanish, throwing her head back and batting her long eyelashes at Mario.

We see the Corderos often, and when Aimee visits, she is always included in whatever we have planned together. It is as though Aimee has her own fan club and social network when she comes to San Jose. Whenever she meets people she hasn't seen in months she always remembers exactly who they are and greets them by name.

One evening we were invited along with the Corderos for an adult-only dinner at the home of some friends, Lou and Nella, who are from Italy. Always very particular and keen on social protocol, they never included children in their adult social activities unless they were specifically invited, which was rare. On this particular occasion, Janise had had an unexpected death in her family and asked if I could take Aimee for the weekend. Under the circumstances, I agreed and telephoned Nella to cancel our dinner plans. I knew her feeling about children tagging along uninvited and therefore preferred not to bring Aimee.

She insisted that we come and bring Aimee with us. Then she wanted to know what she had to prepare for Aimee to eat. "Nothing," I said, "Aimee doesn't need to eat anything special. She will eat whatever is served." Nella was already impressed. She did not know Aimee well and avoided discussions about her. I think it made her uncomfortable. In fact, Nella bristled at anyone who talked about grandchildren too often or too much. She had two bachelor sons at that time and no grandchildren and wasn't particularly interested in talking about kids. Knowing this, I kept my conversation about my grandchildren to a minimum. In the presence of the Corderos, though, who always asked about Aimee, Nella would listen.

We arrived at Nella's home as scheduled and enjoyed cocktails outdoors in the beautifully landscaped courtyard. Aimee immediately remembered Lou and Nella and greeted them by name. "Hi, Lou, Hi, Nella, how are you?" she said. And, of course, she responded with joy and affection when the Corderos arrived. Aimee always knows when Myriam arrives by her perfume, jangling bracelets, and distinct accent. Aimee absolutely delighted in Myriam's acknowledgment of her greeting with big hugs and lots of kisses.

Nella, on the other hand, remained somewhat aloof regarding Aimee. I quietly observed Aimee's reaction to this response and it amused me. Aimee kept trying to engage Nella in conversation. Intentionally or not, Nella ignored her and continued her conversation with the adults. Soon, Nella excused herself to tend to her cooking.

Then Aimee said, "Mmmmm, I smell something good cooking." This was followed by a series of comments and questions: "What's Nella cooking in there?" "I like it! I can smell it!" Nella was in the kitchen and I cautiously wheeled Aimee in to smell the food. "Nella, I like it!" "When are we eating?" "What are we eating?"

I could see that Nella was smiling and becoming engaged. Aimee was drawing her in. When dinner was served Aimee sat near Nella. She had perfect manners as I fed her and ate everything on her plate. Nella was in awe and said so. She was even more fascinated when Aimee, smacking her lips, wanted more of Nella's delicious Italian food. Nella took pride in her cooking, and Aimee's sophisticated palate and appreciation of her food impressed her. As is my routine, I took Aimee out of her wheelchair after she finished eating and sat her on my lap. She continued to engage Nella.

"Nella, I like your house," she said. "Where's Lou, what's he doing now?" Soon she said, "Nella, can I sit with you, can I sit on your lap, please?" Nella didn't know how to respond, but she couldn't say no. She looked at me. I said it was totally up to her to do so and only if she felt comfortable. She reluctantly and awkwardly took Aimee on her lap. Aimee is difficult to hold at first, because you must adjust to her position and balance her on your lap. She becomes stiff and leans too far back if not held firmly in place.

Aimee immediately won her over. I watched as Nella's heart softened under Aimee's spell. Nella began to gently stroke Aimee's hand, then her face. Aimee responded by putting her face very close to Nella so she could see her and said, "Nella, I love you!" She wanted to kiss her and threw several of her familiar "air" kisses at Nella. Nella laughed in response and I saw tears well up in her eyes. Then she hugged and kissed Aimee and they laughed and talked more.

Nella told me later that she had never understood how I related to Aimee. In tears, she told me that Aimee had given her a gift by teaching her that handicapped children are special. She never knew how delightful and beautiful a child Aimee was until she opened her heart. Aimee was welcome in their home any time, she said. They had become friends.

On a later trip to Poland, while visiting a cathedral there and lighting candles, Aimee suddenly blurted out, "I have to light a candle for Nella!" We were amazed at Aimee's request because we had only recently learned that Nella was seriously ill and knew that Aimee could have no way of knowing that, and yet, she had remembered Nella.

• • •

Another holiday season rolled around. I had not forgotten about *The Nutcracker* ballet incident the year before, and this time Mel and I would take the twins together. Mel bought front-row tickets for the event. If Aimee couldn't tolerate the environment, he would leave with her. I would remain with Chloe so as not to jeopardize her enjoyment of the performance. The twins were visiting for the weekend and Aimee repeatedly expressed her excitement about attending the ballet. We had read the book several times, and I had given her the CD weeks earlier to familiarize herself with the music. I explained that there would be many children like her and Chloe attending the performance and that "theater manners" were required inside. I explained in detail what to expect as part of the theater and performance. I explained about the aisles, the seats, the lighting, the orchestra, and most important, the reason for applause. I assured her I would help her clap her hands along with everyone else when it was time and that the purpose of clapping was a way to communicate praise to the performers for their talent. She understood.

We ate lunch at a favorite downtown restaurant and walked to the Performing Arts Center. The girls were adorable in their matching navy velvet dresses, black tights, and patent leather Mary Janes. Wearing ribbons in their hair and dress coats with velvet collars, they looked like a pair of dolls. We parked Aimee's wheelchair in the exit aisle and Mel carried her to her seat. Chloe explained everything that was going to happen and held Aimee's hand for reassurance. Their excitement was palpable. The music began and Aimee listened intently to the familiar overture. The audience suddenly broke out in loud applause. I grabbed Aimee's hands before she could respond negatively and helped her clap. She was startled but okay. Then, she got the idea. She continued to listen to the music with intensity and concentration. Except for the movement and lights on the stage, I didn't know what, if anything, she could see. She sat up so straight that we had to balance her on the edge of her seat. She was in awe and she loved it. During intermission she told me that she "heard" the dancers on the stage as they moved with the music. Regardless of how much she could see or not, I knew she enjoyed it immensely. The scope of her pleasure was confirmed when at the end, she yelled, "Bravo! Bravo! Bravo!" at the top of her lungs.

It had been a successful outing. Mel and I were relieved and impressed with Aimee's behavior. Of course, Chloe had set an outstanding example for her sister to follow. They both had a wonderful time and, for once, it was one of those rare occasions where they could actually do something special together.

• • •

Aimee spent the week with us between Christmas and New Year's Day. We received an invitation from a longtime family friend to join them for brunch at their home. It was a family event and they wanted our children to come too. No one was available on such short notice, so we accepted the invitation and took Aimee along. Bill, our host, a retired psychoanalyst, knew Aimee and was impressed with her improved cognitive ability and social skills. He took Aimee around and introduced her to the other children, in particular, his granddaughter and a great-niece. Aimee attempted to connect with them immediately but they were absorbed in play and ignored her. When lunch was served, I prepared Aimee's plate and sat her next to me near Bill and Mel. I had to feed her, and this caught the attention of the great-niece, a precocious eight-year-old. She walked up to me, hands on her hips, and asked, "Why does she have to act that way?" Aimee remembered her name and said, "Hi, Rachael, what are you doing? Come closer so I can see you. Come over here." She ignored Aimee and continued with her questions. "Why does she talk like that?" Before I could answer, she asked, "What's wrong with her?" Her tone was sharp and condescending, even as I patiently answered her questions. "Why do you have to feed her? Can't she feed herself?"

I knew she was just a child, but I didn't appreciate her attitude. Many children ask about Aimee and they are curious about her condition, sometimes frightened of her wheelchair, and often stare. I wholeheartedly and sincerely encourage their questions and view it as an opportunity to educate them. She, on the other hand, was clearly appalled at Aimee's condition and her presence at the party.

Aimee picked up on this immediately. She wasn't going to allow herself to be intimidated. She turned to me and said, "Grammy, Grammy, look at me. I want to show her how strong I am!" She pushed her feet down on her footrests and pushed herself up. She lifted her arms to display her strength and she made a mighty sigh to exaggerate her power. Aimee was in control and she wanted Rachael to know it in no uncertain terms. I reassured her that she was a strong girl and I was proud of her for it. In spite of all her limitations, she understood and had made her point. I loved her for the confidence and poise with which she seized the moment to display her inner and outer strength.

Others see these qualities and are drawn to her. Impressed with her social prowess, complete strangers often want to touch her head, hold her hand, or hug her. Aimee's charisma often solicits well-wishers and pledges to pray for her. Complete strangers often call her an "angel."

• • •

One such occasion occurred at the Saks Fifth Avenue store then located in Carmel, California. Aimee was spending the weekend with us at our beach house, and we took a drive to Carmel to enjoy lunch and a leisurely afternoon. While in town, I wanted to look around Saks. I selected a coat and put it on hold while we did some other shopping. A couple of hours later, we returned to Saks to buy the coat. As soon as we entered the store, an attractive woman approached us with a sense of urgency and identified herself as the store manager. She explained that she had watched us on the security monitor when we were in the store earlier in the day. She was "enchanted" by Aimee and couldn't resist approaching us now. She had been waiting for our return. Asking permission to talk with Aimee, she knelt down beside her and held her hand, exclaiming, "I had to touch this angel." With tears rolling down her cheeks she thanked us for the opportunity to meet Aimee and said she would remember her in her prayers.

• • •

Family members were also not immune to Aimee's charisma; she worked her magic spell on us all. She sensed when someone avoided her and targeted them with an arrow straight to their heart. Such was the case with my ex-husband, Jim, known fondly as "Papa" to Aimee. He remained quite distanced from Aimee from the beginning and seemed to focus more on Chloe. I remembered his reaction at the hospital soon after Aimee's birth and always felt that deep down he was afraid to become too close, to love too much. He felt vulnerable and didn't want to be caught in Aimee's web.

He rarely held Aimee, talked to her, or interacted with her in any way. He continually chastised me for giving what he believed to be false hope to our son and daughter-in-law by taking Aimee for therapy. He criticized Jason for allowing us to make the trips, and he thought it was a useless waste of time and money. "Why can't you just accept her the way she is?" he asked me. I would repeatedly respond with the same answer. "Because I cannot just accept that and, besides, she deserves more."

Our divorce had been hostile and left us both bitter. While our children were in high school and in college, we had little contact with each other. As the years passed our communication improved—but some things didn't change. If I encouraged it, he discouraged it. Taking Aimee to Europe for therapy was no exception and had become the frosting on the cake. He made his feelings known to the family and ridiculed me on numerous occasions. But, in time, Aimee would change that.

When the twins were born, we were all at the hospital. Their birth brought us together and we stayed together most of the afternoon waiting for a report about Aimee. We were together when the unimaginable prognosis was delivered. At the time, Jason was devastated and Jim was there to support him. I appreciated that and talked with Jim when he came to visit Aimee. He was clearly overwhelmed and gravely concerned about how Jason would manage. He looked at Aimee and shook his head as he walked away with his head down. He returned to visit the second day when I was holding Aimee in the rocking chair and feeding her. When he approached I said, "Come sit here. You can hold her." He reluctantly took hold of her, held her little hand, and began to sob. I cried with him. It was a tender moment and I knew he was having as difficult a time coping as the rest of us. He thanked me for being there and left.

That was the first sign I had that Aimee would be the catalyst to restoring our friendship. We would see each other again on the occasion of the twin's baptism a few months later. A quiet celebration was hosted at my home. At that time, Jason, Janise, and the twins had recently moved into our guesthouse. Jim had refused to come there to visit but agreed to come to the party. Fortunately, Mel got along well with Jim, as I did with Jim's wife, Gail. We were classmates all through elementary school and I had known her for many years.

When Jason moved away to Modesto, Jim and I had more in common. We both missed our son and had hoped that our grandchildren would grow up in the San Jose area where Jason had been raised. This established mutual ground between us. When Jason and his family came to San Jose, regardless of the occasion or who extended the primary invitation, we each wanted to visit. Therefore, over time, we learned to share our visits. Forced to coordinate our efforts, often through our daughter, we could no longer remain indifferent to each other and often arranged breakfasts or dinners together. We both loved our son and clearly understood his need for our support. We were forced into civility.

On these occasions, we had lively conversations and lots of laughs. Jim was jovial and good-humored, but sometimes he cut to the quick, using his sharp wit to make his point. His disparaging remarks often hurt, but I took them in stride. When the need arose, he and his wife typically babysat Chloe, while Mel and I babysat Aimee. Aimee attempted to relate to "Papa," but he appeared uncomfortable in her presence. When eating meals together he would focus solely on Chloe, while I fed Aimee. I noticed that he watched me but never offered to do the job.

Janna, our daughter, was interested and curious about Aimee's therapy and became more involved after witnessing firsthand exactly what Aimee did. She was touched and impressed by Aimee's diligence and desire to succeed. Janna shared this information with her father, who still refused to believe it. She mentioned to Jim that I was taking Aimee to Anaheim for another four-week session in January and that she was planning to join us for three or four days.

He continued to criticize until I had finally had enough and suggested to Janna that perhaps Jim would like to come to Anaheim with her to see things for himself. She thought it was a marvelous idea and invited her dad to make the trip with her. I welcomed their participation with enthusiasm and encouraged them to take part in Aimee's therapy with me. Jim, even though he was coming, remained negative and full of skepticism.

The morning after they arrived, I took them to the center, where they remained with Aimee and assisted with her therapy. I intentionally left to do errands. When I returned, I saw Jim reading to Aimee while she was strapped in the stander. I had one more errand to do and had to leave again, and Jim asked if he could join me. Our time together gave him a chance to say what I never thought I'd hear: He admitted he was wrong and said he now understood the value of the therapy and its impact on Aimee's life. He thanked me. I was touched by his words and appreciated his honesty. I knew it was difficult for him to say what he felt.

Valentine's Day was coming and I wanted to buy treats to bring to the children. He thought it was a great idea and said, "Let's do it now. I'd like to help." I was surprised.

I prepared lunch for us in our hotel suite and we visited all afternoon. By then, Aimee was enamored with "Papa" and enjoying his attention. We all went to Downtown Disney for ice cream and later for pizza before returning to our hotel room.

Aimee wanted to show him everything she could do. I put her on the floor so she could show how she could "crawl." It was one of the rare times when she actually was able to get up on her hands and knees. He clapped and hollered cheers for her. She was thrilled! For the second time I witnessed him turn away in tears, as he had done five years earlier at her birth. He was touched when she wanted him to sing and dance with her. During this time, Elvis was Aimee's idol. She listened to his music incessantly and memorized every song. She sang, ate, and slept to Elvis. She couldn't get enough. When Jim danced with her to "Blue Suede Shoes," she exploded with laughter and joy.

We ate breakfast together in the morning before saying our good-byes at the airport. Jim and I hugged tight, sharing unspoken words of appreciation for the wonderful days shared with the grandchild we both loved. After years of being at odds with each other, this little girl had brought us together.

When they called later that day to say they had arrived home, Jim recalled with humor Aimee's obsession with everything Elvis. He called again later that evening and pretended to be Elvis, making his voice sound like the King. Aimee believed him and shook with delight and began to cry with excitement when she thought it was really Elvis on the phone.

The weekend was a success and was one of Jim's favorite times, and mine too. We laughed, cried, and enjoyed the company of our daughter and granddaughter together. Five months later, we were all devastated when Jim suddenly and unexpectedly died of complications from diabetes. The night before he passed away, Aimee told her mother that she saw him in her sleep. She said, "Papa came to tell me good-bye and to always be a happy girl in my wheelchair." He died the next day. Aimee prevailed and won his heart. We knew he was at peace.

THE POWER OF LOVE

AIMEE CONTINUED TO DO WELL in her special classes at school. Her kindergarten/first-grade teacher had cerebral palsy and understood firsthand the needs of her students. She was a disciplinarian and expected Aimee to learn classroom protocol and demonstrate good behavior and manners, which would require a change from Aimee's preference for chatter and laughter. Nevertheless, her teacher confided that she was a joy and a challenge in class. And, in spite of the new rules, Aimee liked her very much.

If Aimee misbehaved in class, she would have a time-out outside the classroom door for a moment or two. Aimee told me that her teacher often said, "Aimee, stop it *immediately*!" It was a word Aimee liked to say often; she loved to mimic her teacher, making me laugh.

We began to suspect that Aimee's limited vision could be the reason for her short attention span in the classroom. At her IEP meeting, it was recommended that we check whether she needed glasses. Janise arranged an appointment at the University of California, San Francisco (UCSF) with a pediatric ophthalmologist. The physician who examined and evaluated her eyesight said Aimee's vision could not be corrected and was a consequence of her brain damage. He told us that her range of sight was comparable to looking through a colander: she had spots of clear vision and areas of no vision at all. He concluded that corrective lenses that magnified the field of sight might help her to focus. We thought it was worth a try. Aimee didn't. She didn't like wearing glasses and pulled them off whenever she could. Now and then, she would request them saying, "I can't see, put on my glasses." Or, "My glasses are in my backpack, please get them for me." I knew she didn't like wearing the glasses all the time but realized that they did help in certain situations. She wore them at school and often at home. When she visited, I left it up to her to tell me if she wanted them on or not. Sometimes, I'd suggest putting on her glasses while watching TV or a movie, and she would agree. In general, it seemed that she preferred to have them off.

Physicians who have examined Aimee have always been impressed with her abilities. One neurologist at UCSF told us that if he had seen Aimee's MRI prior to meeting her, he would never have believed it was the same child. He said he thought it was "pure love" from her family, combined with support and encouragement, that was responsible for Aimee's remarkable success. He also said that she had been given a will to live and a purpose in life to achieve and do her best because she knew she had a place of importance in our family. As he spoke, his voice quivering, my thoughts drifted to all the people who had offered so much love and so many prayers for Aimee. I also believed it was unconditional love and unlimited faith that had brought her so far.

But her challenges continued. One examination with a pediatric orthopedist raised concerns that Aimee was developing scoliosis. He concluded that she would probably require surgery in the future, and we scheduled a return visit for the following year.

During that year, Janise received a letter from the Shriners Hospital for Children in Sacramento. Months earlier she had found an application while looking through a parenting magazine and decided to send it in. Shriners Hospitals for Children is a one-of-a-kind health system, located across the United States, dedicated to helping children with cerebral palsy, burns, and cleft lip in a family-centered environment at no charge. She had forgotten about it until the letter arrived. The letter explained that Aimee was a candidate for their program, and they wanted to schedule an evaluation. Janise invited me to accompany her to Aimee's initial evaluation. We were very pleased to learn that Aimee was accepted into their program and would be eligible for their services until age eighteen. This was wonderful news. Shriners have been a leader in providing orthopedic care to children since 1922.

The initial evaluation at Shriners and subsequent follow-up visits confirmed that, as a result of scoliosis, Aimee needed hip surgery, and soon. We were all concerned. Her right hip was almost 30 percent out of the socket. It required correction. Without surgery, her back would continue to worsen and cause long-term damage. The doctor provided us with a detailed explanation of the procedure. Recovery would be the most difficult and would take eight to twelve weeks, during which time she would be in a full body cast. We knew it needed to be done and I knew her parents would do what was best for Aimee.

Aimee and I spent some time together before the surgery, and she overheard us talking about it. It didn't appear to have any effect on her, even when we told her about the cast. We concluded that she probably didn't understand. But I continued to worry that the surgery would be traumatic for her and went so far as to call my friend Bill, a retired psychotherapist, to ask his advice. He advised that we be honest and straightforward and tell her exactly what was going to take place even if she appeared not to comprehend. Jason later told me that he had explained in detail to Aimee that she was going to the hospital to have "surgery" and that she would have a "cast." He was confident she understood and I was relieved that he had explained it to her.

I packed my bags and headed for Modesto to pick up Janise and Aimee. Mel and Jason would join us in Sacramento that evening. The hotel, located near the UC Davis Medical Center and Shriners Hospital campus, was both comfortable and convenient. Our plans changed slightly when Janise decided to drive her own car. Aimee wanted to ride with me and I was pleased to have her join me. We listened to music during the hour and a half drive to Sacramento. About halfway there, Aimee said, "Grammy, I have a question."

"Okay," I said, "what's your question?"

"What does it mean to have *surgery*?" she asked. Just like that. She wanted to know and was asking me to explain. What do I say now? I recalled Bill's advice and I knew I had to be truthful and direct. Aimee trusted me, and I didn't want to let her down. She had a right to know what to expect, but I didn't want to frighten her.

I wanted to make it sound fun—but not too fun. I explained that we were going to the hotel first to check in and would have dinner with Aunt Janna, who lived near Sacramento. Aimee understood from experience that going to a hotel with Grammy meant a good time. Then I plunged in. In the morning we would take her to the hospital where we would all stay with her until the surgery; I said we would all be there and would not leave her no matter what. After they examined her they would give her medicine to help her go to sleep so she wouldn't feel anything. While she was sleeping, the doctor would do the surgery, which meant he would make a cut on her right hip and see inside so he could fix it. After that, they would wrap her all up, real tight and hard, in something called a cast. It would keep her from being able to move. She would have a cast for a long time so her hip could heal and then it would come off. It wouldn't hurt her, but it would be uncomfortable. When the doctor finished with the surgery he would wake her up and she would see us all again.

Then she asked, "What does it mean to stay in the hospital?" I explained that it was similar to a hotel, except that it was for children to stay while they were waiting to get better. I told her that her mother would stay with her all night and that she would not be alone. When she was well enough, the doctor would let her go home and I would be there for a week, just to take care of her, feed her lots of ice cream, and play with her. She liked that, smiled, and seemed to be fine with my answer. We talked a little more about it and I assured her she would be safe. I asked her if she understood what I told her, and she said she did.

The conversation made me feel relieved, then tearful. It was clear to me that Aimee was aware and concerned about what was going to happen to her. Her appropriate questions left me worried about her tolerance of the entire process. She had suffered so much already; I didn't want her to suffer more.

By now, it came as no surprise to see Aimee work the room and bond with the nurses when we arrived. But I was surprised at how well she was doing. When the doctor came in to greet her and ask about her favorite colors for the cast, she said "Purple! No, no, no, pink!" Finally he said, "Okay Aimee, I'll make it purple *and* pink." She liked that and laughed. I could only imagine what a purple and pink cast would look like. Surely he was joking. Didn't they do white casts anymore?

Aimee's surgery was delayed for several hours. We arrived at 7:00 a.m. and it was now past noon. She hadn't had anything to eat since dinner the evening before and was hungry. We waited longer. Finally, her doctor, his assistant, and the anesthesiologist entered the room in their surgical attire. Aimee knew immediately that things were different. They were serious now. Her lips quivered; she stiffened and began to shake uncontrollably and cry. They had to hold her down, as she screamed, to start an IV. I felt terrible and left the room holding back tears of my own. She was so frightened, so helpless, and so frail. When they took her away we all cried. Poor Aimee had already gone through so much.

We waited and watched the clock as the hours dragged by: three, four, and five. I was extremely concerned with her ability to tolerate the anesthetic and wondered if the lengthy period of unconsciousness would cause further trauma to her brain, or worse, seizures. The doctor assured us there should be no problem, but it is hard not to fear what may go wrong. There are always risks.

Finally, after five hours, Aimee's surgeon appeared, smiling as he approached us. This was a relief and hint that good news was forthcoming. He explained the details of the surgery and that it went well. Aimee was in the recovery room and we could see her soon. The nurse would come and get us when she was awake. She was in a body cast from her chest to the tips of her toes.

Soon the nurse arrived and told us we could see her. Jason and Janise went in first and came out in tears with their heads down. We exchanged glances. Mel and I went in next. I was stunned when I saw her. As expected, she was very dopey. The cast was something else. It was purple and pink alternating stripes from top to bottom, similar to a colorful, old-fashioned barber's pole! But for all its cheerful color, it was a sobering sight.

The cast began under her armpits, wrapped around her entire body, and ended at the tips of her toes, exposing only the edge of her toenail. She was totally encased, feet flexed at right angles, legs apart and elevated. It was as if she had been placed in stirrups, plaster casted, and then lifted off the table in that position. Pillows were used to prop up her legs and to support her bent knees while her back remained flat against the bed. The cast was open so she could go to the bathroom, but it would be a very delicate task. As I held Aimee's hand, I studied the cast carefully, wondering how in the world we were going to lift and position her. Feeding, keeping her clean, and especially toileting for the next eight weeks were going to be demanding. She would wear a very large diaper over the cast with padding around the opening at the bottom. This area had to remain absolutely clean to avoid infection or deterioration of the cast. The bilateral abductor muscles in her groin had also been cut and she had stitches that were in close proximity to, but not visible from, the opening. This was going to be a challenge. I was glad I planned to stay in Modesto for a week to help out. Janise would need as much help as her mom and I could give. Now I understood the look on their faces when Jason and Janise came out.

Before we left the recovery room, I kissed Aimee and in a whisper assured her that it was over. She opened her eyes, smiled, and said, "Grammy, I'm stuck!" Her smile was the reassurance I needed that she was okay. This little girl was stronger than I had imagined or given her credit for. She was so full of resolve and determination, I knew she would get through this. We remained with her the rest of the afternoon, left for dinner, and then returned to the hospital. We said goodnight and went to our hotel with Jason. Janise would sleep in Aimee's room. At 3:00 a.m., we were startled awake when the phone rang. It was Janise.

In tears, she asked me to come to the hospital. "Julie, could you stay with Aimee until morning?" She was at her limit, exhausted and upset. Aimee had been crying all night. "Of course," I said, "I'll be right there." I dressed and walked to the hospital. Aimee was in pain and Janise was spent. I reassured Janise that Aimee would be fine and encouraged her to get some sleep. I comforted Aimee, rubbed her cheeks, and held her hands. She began to relax. Moving slowly, I was able to edge myself onto the folding bed next to hers. She was restless and finally, after receiving pain medication, fell asleep. Now, I was the one who couldn't sleep.

The following day was the same. Mel and I alternated with Jason and Janise so that someone was always at Aimee's side. She was wide awake and talking, but still in a great deal of pain. I stayed with her again that night and finally slept. Janise stayed with her on Sunday night. Mel and Jason headed for home. We were encouraged to remain at the hospital until we felt comfortable taking her home, so we decided to stay another night and left the hospital Monday morning.

Janise was concerned about Aimee's care. We listened carefully to the instructions from the doctor and watched attentively as the nurse demonstrated hygiene and cleansing requirements. We were given written instructions as well. Aimee could not sit up or use her regular wheelchair. Instead, Janise had made arrangements through her local regional center for an adult-sized wheelchair with extended leg supports, which would be used during Aimee's recovery so that she could remain flat on her back. Multiple pillows were positioned to support her in her cast so that she could be turned from side to side and elevated to eat. The hospital loaned us a harness-type seatbelt to position her on her side in the car.

Lifting Aimee in the cast was difficult. Generally it was easier if she faced out, away from you, when being held. If you held her toward you, she had to be positioned sideways against your chest with one leg sticking up and out. When propped up to eat, her legs had to be supported. In bed, she had to be positioned with pillows under her leg so she could lie on her back. To ride in the car, she had to lie across the backseat on her side with pillows supporting her leg in the air.

In her large wheelchair, lying flat with pillows stuffed around her, she could be moved from room to room. She made it known exactly where she wanted to be and bossed us around to get her there.

By the end of the first week, we had mastered our techniques and gained confidence in caring for her. Janise would manage fine without me. I assured her that as soon as Aimee was stable and out of pain, I would give her a few days of relief by bringing Aimee to San Jose. It was going to be a long eight weeks.

We took her back to Shriners Hospital for her checkup three weeks later. We were impressed with her understanding of the process and her positive attitude throughout the recovery period. To her credit, Aimee tolerated the cast without complaint. In fact, after only three weeks, she was asking to return to school and with the doctor's approval was able to do so. Janise drove her to school, where she remained, lying on her back and propped in her big wheelchair but happy to be with her friends.

Mel and I were able to take Aimee for two weekends during her recovery period. As was our tradition, we spent Thanksgiving with Mel's brother Ron and his wife, Joan. Janise asked me earlier if we could babysit Aimee so that they could attend a special family reunion over the Thanksgiving weekend. I said yes, but only if it was agreeable to Ron and Joan. They adored Aimee and she happily came along, cast and all.

Aimee made our Thanksgiving extra special that year and we marveled at her chatter and humor as she entertained us from her big wheelchair. The cast had become routine by now, and we were used to the adult diapers, oversized clothes, and candy-cane purple and pink stripes. She was quite a sight but adorable as always.

Ron and Joan enjoyed Aimee so much that year that she has been included in their Thanksgiving invitation every year since. Joan's long-time friend Doris, a former nun, also was a guest. She read to Aimee and they talked quietly about God. Aimee continued to work the room and was cunning in planning her strategy for attention.

Aimee asked Joan about everything on the menu and tasted it all. She requested that Ron take her outside at least once an hour to smell the turkey roasting on the Weber grill. When dinner was served, she flattered them with her comments about the food and ate the delicious meal with zest and enthusiasm.

Ron and Joan's only son had died ten years earlier. Thanksgiving, near the anniversary date of his death, was sad and difficult for them. Aimee brought a spark of light into this dark time for them. When she called Joan "Grammy Joan," we all choked up. No one told her to do so, but perhaps she somehow understood that Joan would never have grandchildren of her own. Aimee illustrated the true spirit of Thanksgiving that day by embracing her gifts and sharing her love and appreciation of life with us all.

She remained with us one more weekend while in her cast. Visiting our home meant she could expect the royal treatment and lots of attention. It was amazing how she had accommodated the body cast and maintained a positive attitude for her entire recovery. I developed a new respect for her courage and determination to overcome this obstacle. I loved and admired her so much.

At last the eight weeks came to an end. Skinny to begin with, Aimee had lost a considerable amount of weight by December. The cast was literally hanging on her weak and frail body. It would be off before the New Year and we couldn't wait. We returned to Shriners for the cast removal and were eager to see it go. She lay still as the blade cut the cast but began to shake when it was being released. When it was finally removed, and her body released from its hold, the unfamiliar sensation brought her to tears. She had been an inspiration to all who witnessed her valor and indefatigable spirit, but we were glad this chapter was finally over.

STUDENT OF THE MONTH

THE HIP SURGERY was a powerful experience for Aimee, even at age seven. Her maturity, self-awareness, and confidence seemed to grow even more. She was doing well at school and had finally mastered classroom protocol, especially learning not to interrupt.

Aimee is eager to learn and responds especially well to auditory stimulation. With music, she studies the instruments, the melody, and the rhythm. With books, she turns the pages and memorizes the characters, if not the story itself. She always wants to know who wrote and illustrated the book and will remember the next time we read it to her. Her favorite adventures include going to the book and music store or, more recently, visiting iTunes on the computer.

We often spent hours at the bookstore exploring and reading new books to buy. One day, while wandering the aisles, I noticed a black book with white letters and next to it a white book with black letters. Curious, I picked them up and wondered if Aimee could see them. I showed her the books. She had no response to the book with the black images. But when I showed her the book with white images on black pages, she quickly pointed to an image and said, "Teddy bear." "Aimee, can you see that?" I asked. As I turned the pages, she couldn't identify all the images, but she could see them. The book was quite infantile, but I bought it anyway. I wanted to test her at home to determine if she could actually make out shapes and characters.

My brain was in high gear as I began to think about what this meant. If she could see white on black, it meant she might be able to identify letters of the alphabet and shapes. I tested her more. She was also enthusiastic and excited as we began to play a game. I cut out shapes from white paper and placed them on black construction paper. She was able to identify every one. "Wow!" I said, "Good for you, Aimee!" She shouted out the names of the shapes with joy and confidence. "Square!" "Triangle!" "Circle!" "Heart!"

I mixed them around, thinking that she had already memorized them in order, but she knew them no matter what order they were presented. I continued to cut more shapes: a tree, a car, a boat, a house, a dinosaur, an apple, and more. We were on a roll! She identified every item. I was astonished at what she knew. All this knowledge, I thought, has been trapped in her mind with no outlet. How much more is in there? I wondered. She was thrilled with her accomplishment, and so was I.

When Mel came home, we showed him. I put Aimee through the exercise again. I mixed up the items once more and she identified them all. She shouted loudly as she proudly named each item, "House!" "Apple!" "Boat!"

"Is Tutu listening?" she asked.

"I'm listening, Aimee."

She was so proud of herself that she exclaimed, "Come on, Aimee, you can do it!" Then in her singsong voice she said, "Good j-o-o-o-o-b!" We laughed.

I asked her if she would like me to make her a book with pictures. "I want a book, I want a book," she replied. What a breakthrough. I thought about making a book for her with pictures, shapes, letters, and numbers. Encouraged by her ability, and artistically motivated, I went to the local copy store where they knew me well. I explained in detail what I wanted to accomplish, and they made me several small books of thick black paper bound with spiral bands. I cut out more shapes on white paper and glued them in the book. Then I went to the office supply store where I purchased large 4-inch white letters and put them in another book. I worked on the books all evening.

The next morning, when Aimee saw her books for the first time, she was delighted. We reviewed them over and over as I changed the order of the pictures. I wanted to be certain she didn't memorize the order. We couldn't wait to show her parents what she could do.

"Watch! Listen to me!" Aimee exclaimed to her parents. "Are you listening?" Then we began and she shouted out the identity of items on the page. The other children wanted the book, too, so we shared. I was firm, however, in making it understood that these were one-of-a-kind books made especially for Aimee. I remained adamant that they were not to be taken away from her under any circumstances, as was often done with other books. I explained that they were to remain in her backpack where she wanted them to be. This was difficult because Chloe and Jeffrey saw something new, different, and special and wanted it, too. Janise always encourages them to share everything, which I respect. But when it came to Aimee's toys, books, and favorite music, it became an issue.

Educational toys and items appropriate for Aimee are very difficult to find and require careful consideration and research. Mel and I spend hours looking through special-needs catalogs and stores for just the right item. The other children usually received the special items they want for their birthdays and holidays. Aimee, however, cannot request something that she does not know exists, other than books or music. We must present ideas and concepts to her in other creative ways, often with handmade toys or special-order items. Her siblings do not always understand this and, because they are children, often want what she is given. This is a dilemma for Mel and me. The special books, for example, took hours of time to create. I hated restricting the other children but hoped they would be considerate and respect my wishes. This has been a difficult lesson for them to learn.

What Aimee can and cannot see remains somewhat of a mystery. When she looks in the mirror, she frequently comments that she sees

Chloe. Sometimes she recognizes herself. And sometimes she will say that she and Chloe "have the same face," which they do. I always explain that they are identical twins and that's why they look the same. I'm not sure she understands what twins are, but she clearly understands that Chloe is her "sissy" and loves her. Aimee also notices and comments on faces and their shapes. "Tutu has a big face," she told me one day. Mel is Japanese and does have a round face. I laughed. After touching and feeling my face, she exclaimed, "Grammy, you have a nice face and your hair sticks up!" I must have been having a bad hair day.

Aimee has no problem regularly expressing her needs and wishes. When visiting, she requests that we eat a particular type of food or at a certain restaurant in town. She especially likes Chinese and Italian food. Her favorite store, of course, is Barnes & Noble. Aimee, so good at manipulating, is able to manipulate us too. I finally figured out that her desire to continually go to Max's Restaurant was because there was a Barnes & Noble bookstore in the same complex. When she visits, Aimee wants to know everything we have planned for the day and wants to do it all. She considers her input important, and it is.

• • •

One day in January of 2004, Chloe called to ask if I could come to her school at 8:00 a.m. that Friday for Grandparent's Day. I was pleased that Chloe wanted to include me in this important class activity and wouldn't have missed it for the world. A couple of days prior to that, however, Janise had called to tell me that Aimee was being awarded "Student of the Month" at her school on that same Friday morning. Aimee's assembly was at 10:00 a.m.

I drove to Modesto Thursday night and checked in at my hotel. It was too risky taking a chance on the traffic. I wanted to be there on time. Chloe attended Catholic school, and when she invited me she didn't understand that grandparents were invited to attend a mass with the children as part of the "Grandparent's Day" celebration. The mass was scheduled for 10:00 a.m., the same time as Aimee's event. I planned to attend the first part of the program but regretted having to miss the mass. This was one of those times when I felt torn between both girls. A choice had to be made. It saddened me to leave Chloe and I explained the best I could. I hoped she understood. I love both girls and these situations are heart-wrenching for me. Jackie, Chloe's other grandmother, remained with Chloe for the mass portion of the morning.

I would be the only guest at Aimee's school to witness her receiving her award. I didn't want her to receive it alone, but I still felt guilty leaving Chloe. I arrived at the school early. Aimee's teacher was pleased to see me and explained that Aimee did not know she was getting an award. She hoped that Aimee would tolerate the assembly and not have to be removed from the auditorium, as often was the case because of the clapping. The teacher encouraged me to explain to Aimee that she was receiving an award that day.

I took Aimee to a quiet corner. "I'm so happy to see you, Grammy," she said. I told her I was happy to see her, too, and explained that I would be attending her assembly that morning. I told her in detail, using simple terms, that she was receiving an award and was being honored for being a special student at school.

"What does it mean to award?" she asked. I explained that she was being recognized for her accomplishments. I told her that it was an honor and that she should be proud and sit up tall and strong in her chair when they called her name. I knew she would understand the concept of being "strong." We practiced clapping together and I encouraged her to clap with the other children when they clapped for something or someone. I told her that all the children would be clapping just for her when they called her name, which meant they were happy for her and proud of her, too. She listened intently, but I didn't know if she understood it all. I had to wait and see.

I took a seat near the stage and waited, feeling a tinge of nostalgia as I recalled so many memories of my own children and similar events at their schools. Soon the children filed in, grade by grade, classroom by classroom. The kids in wheelchairs were pushed by their "amigos," other students in higher grades who volunteer to assist them. I was openly moved when I saw Aimee enter with her group—balloons tied to her chair, smiling, she was being pushed by her own "amigo" from the fifth-grade class.

Things quieted down and soon the assembly program began. The principal welcomed everyone and explained that the purpose of the program that morning was to present special awards to those students who had accomplished "something remarkable." Each grade level had one student, nominated and selected by the teachers, who was receiving the coveted "Student of the Month Award." Aimee had attended school in her body cast, was eager to learn, and had made improvements in self-control. She had inspired her teacher and was selected for the award. She deserved it, without a doubt.

Aimee was jubilant at being wheeled on stage with other recipients when her name was announced. I was ecstatic but held my breath, hoping she wouldn't start to cry. Each recipient was praised for his or her individual accomplishments and presented with an award. As each award was announced, the children hooted, howled, and clapped. Aimee laughed and screamed with them. No tears. She was actually participating. I was so happy for her.

It was Aimee's turn to receive the award. Everyone stood, applauded, and yelled. Aimee screamed and clapped the best she could along with the others. Faculty, teachers, and peers honored her with a standing ovation. Aimee's teacher had told me in the past that Aimee was very popular, but now I saw it for myself. I couldn't believe the impact this little girl had on others. My heart swelled and tears of joy filled my eyes. It was a moment of fulfillment for me. Aimee had come full circle. To be part of this moment in her life, and to witness her jubilation, surpassed any other experience I had shared with her in the past. I would never forget this special day.

Aimee's teacher, who had positioned herself in close proximity to Aimee, was crying, truly touched. She approached me, held my hand, and told me how much this event meant to her. She said this was the first time Aimee hadn't cried during the applause. It was a huge achievement on Aimee's part. I was pleased to hear her words of praise, although I was not surprised. I've always known in my heart that Aimee has the ability and the will to accomplish the impossible. At the conclusion of the program, everyone gathered around Aimee to congratulate her.

It had been one of those spiritual moments, when I felt the power of divine intervention in Aimee's presence. I thanked God for His gift.

THE HEART ATTACK

I AWOKE AROUND 2:00 A.M. It was dark and quiet in the hotel room. I couldn't shake my feeling of gloom. I had dreamed about my friend of many years and a wave of melancholy came over me. I had first met Bill over thirty-five years ago when he interviewed me for a position in his medical group. "Can you type?" he asked. That was the extent of the interview and I had landed the job that lasted over eighteen years and a treasured friendship that lasted long beyond that. Bill had been my confidant and mentor throughout the years and I viewed him with the highest level of admiration and respect. Now, in real life, he had been very ill for some time. In my dream, however, he was a young man in his thirties as he had been when we first met. Handsome and direct, he sat at a big table across from me and said, "Julie! Julie wake up! You must wake up; you're having a stroke or a heart attack! Wake up!"

I was hundreds of miles from home and alone with Aimee. It was the first week of another month-long therapy session in Anaheim, and the first following Aimee's surgery.

It had been a difficult day for Aimee. The arm exercises made her wince and scream in pain. It had been a difficult day for me too. I knew she was hurting and finally asked the therapists to stop. It was too emotional for me and I felt terrible for Aimee. I could see that she wanted to do it but simply could not perform. She wanted ice cream after therapy and although that treat was reserved for after lunch, I took her anyway. Considering the circumstances, who cared? She had earned it and could eat her lunch later. We talked and relaxed as we ate our ice cream and then returned to our hotel.

Aimee went to bed early. I talked with Mel and went to bed exhausted.

. . .

Now I was awake and knew something was wrong. How odd that I should dream about Bill, I thought to myself. I wondered why he would tell me I was sick even if it was only in a dream. I sat up and thought about the dream for a few minutes and then tried to go back to sleep. It was impossible. Every time I tried to lie down I felt pressure in my chest and back. I remained in a sitting position and began to acknowledge that I did not feel that great. In fact, I was beginning not to feel well at all. I propped the pillows behind me and sat up in bed, hands folded in my lap waiting, I suppose, to feel better. Suddenly, I remembered the popcorn I had eaten right before bedtime. Of course, it was the popcorn, I thought. It must have given me indigestion. I got out of bed to find the wrapper and check the expiration date, but there was none on the package. I very rarely have indigestion. Still, I took an antacid that was in the pharmacopoeia Mel had prepared for me for the month in case of emergency. It didn't help. I went back to bed where I continued to sit and wait. What could be wrong?

Over an hour had passed and it was 3:30 a.m. I couldn't sleep. I put my head back and closed my eyes and rested. I waited until 4:30 a.m. and decided to call Mel and get his opinion. I knew he would be up by then because he goes to his office early. He answered on the second ring and immediately asked what was wrong.

"I don't know; I just don't feel right. Something is wrong, but I cannot pinpoint what it is!" I said. I explained about the popcorn and he, too, was certain it was a case of indigestion. He told me not to worry and recommended that I prepare a slice of toast and try to eat something. He thought it would settle my stomach. I thought perhaps it could be my gallbladder. "Don't people feel like they have indigestion when it's their gallbladder?" I asked.

If it were true, he thought I would have more pain. I agreed to eat toast and call him again in an hour or so. I did not want him to call me because I didn't want the phone to wake Aimee. She needed her rest. I quietly got out of bed again and made a slice of toast and took a bite. The room began to spin, I saw red shards and lines in front my eyes. My hands were wet and clammy. Chills came over me and I felt dizzy. Something was wrong, but I had no idea what.

Our door was locked from the inside with a bolt. What if I faint? What would happen to Aimee? She cannot get out of bed or use the phone to call for help. Who would hear her cries? I decided to unlock the door. Then I returned to bed, where I sat resting against the pillows.

I wondered if I should call the front desk; perhaps they had a physician on call? I waited a little longer, then called the hotel. There was no doctor on-site, but they did have a physician who could come to the hotel if necessary. I wrote down his number and called. It was around 5:00 a.m. He listened to my complaints and encouraged me to call him again after 9:00 a.m. If I still felt ill he would come out then. I agreed to call him back and hung up.

I became more and more uncomfortable as the pressure between my shoulder blades grew. I got up and dressed myself but returned to bed dizzy and weak. Seriously concerned, I got up again and opened the door to our suite, leaving it slightly ajar. Certainly someone would hear Aimee and come inside if anything happened to me. Frightened at that thought, I decided to wake Aimee. I changed her diaper and dressed her. I was simply too weak and dizzy to brush her teeth or comb her hair. It would have to wait.

Groggy with sleep and only partially awake, she cooperated and smiled at me. I kissed her and told her that I did not feel well. I explained to her that I was "sick" but that I didn't want her to be scared. I wanted her to be brave and "trust" me no matter what. This was a new word I had been teaching her about for some time. She understood what it meant to trust and I needed her to know she could trust me now.

She responded with, "Okay, Grammy, I understand." Then she asked, "What does it mean to be sick? Are you sick?" At that point I was failing fast and I knew it. I had to sit down but I needed to get her into her wheelchair first. I did not want her to be alone, in bed, if I fainted. I barely managed to lift her off the bed. Finally, she was in her chair and I strapped her in.

I could no longer stand. I pulled her chair close as I collapsed on the sofa. "Aimee," I said, "Grammy is very, very ill but don't get scared, okay?" She told me she wasn't scared. It felt like an elephant was sitting on my chest as I struggled to reach for the phone. I called the front desk and Mike the night manager answered. Barely able to speak, I asked him to come to the room quickly, I told him that I was alone with Aimee and thought I was going to faint. My throat was tightening and I could barely breathe. I knew I was in trouble. Suddenly, I remembered the dream. A heart attack! No, it simply could not be!

Within minutes Mike ran to our room. "I've called an ambulance and they'll be right here!" he shouted. He said he was studying to be a paramedic and, looking at me, said he thought I was having a heart attack. I nodded my head in agreement. I thought so, too. He called 911 again.

I asked him to take care of Aimee. "Please watch her," I said. "She needs to be fed and she can't do anything for herself." Then I turned to Aimee and said, "Aimee, this is Mike and he will watch you. He will take care of you while Grammy is gone. You can *trust* him."

She looked at me, confused, and said, "Okay Grammy, I'm okay."

I told her not to be scared and to be a good girl. I assured her I would be back.

"I like Mike, I like him." she responded.

Thank you, God. Suddenly my cell phone rang and it was Mel. He was cheery and asked if I was feeling better. I had forgotten to call him back and he was concerned. Hardly able to breathe, much less talk, I attempted to answer. "Heart attack I think . . ." I whispered.

"What? That's impossible! You're not having a heart attack!" He continued, "Just get that idea out of your head; you have no symptoms; it's impossible!" I couldn't respond. Mike grabbed the phone out of my hand and told Mel what was happening. At that moment, the paramedics burst into the room. "Oxygen!" one shouted.

Oh, I could breathe again. I turned to Mike and said, "Please watch Aimee and tell my husband what is happening."

"Aimee, I love you, you're a good girl!" I said.

Suddenly I was lifted over the back of the sofa, placed on a gurney, and rushed to the waiting ambulance. I remember the medic's words: "Stay with us, Julie, stay with us! You've had a heart attack!"

I began to pray. Please God, don't let me die. Not now, not this way, and not while Aimee is here alone. Please watch over her and keep her safe. I made deals and promises as I bargained with God for my life. Please God, let me live.

Within minutes we were at a hospital. I was out of it and barely conscious when I was rushed into the emergency room. I remember thinking it must be a very small hospital because the ER had only two or three patient stalls. Where am I?

Nurses and doctors rushed to my side. I was hooked up to monitors, tubes, and oxygen. It all happened so fast. I was in a daze but conscious. I closed my eyes and continued to pray. I thought about Aimee. I thought about my husband, my children, my parents, family, and friends.

The doctor returned and told me that the blood tests confirmed I had suffered a massive heart attack. The cause was apparently a blood clot. I would need a shot immediately of what he called the "blood blaster." There was no time to waste, he explained. I needed to make a decision immediately. It was risky and if it didn't work I could hemorrhage from anywhere and everywhere in my body. If it worked, though, it could save my life and break up any additional clots that could go to my heart or brain. He explained that it needed to happen soon because I had run out of time. I would be required to sign a permit. He excused himself for a minute or two to give me time to think and make my decision.

I was all alone. What should I do? I had to make a decision and thought about what Mel would advise if he were here. I knew my answer. I had to do it.

The doctor returned. "Well?" he asked. When I said yes, he handed me the permit to sign. Terrified and alone, I put my life in God's hands. These could be my final moments I thought, the end of my life. I might never see my family again or live to see tomorrow. I would know soon. I prayed.

• • •

A person of deep faith, I knew my course was already beyond my control. It was out of my hands and in the hands of a higher power. I had so much to live for and still so much to do. My father's own sad disappointed words spoken on his deathbed echoed in my mind. At the end of his life, Domenic had said he still had so much he wanted to do. But I also realized that, like my father, if it were my time to be called home, I would go with a grateful heart for the wonderful life I had lived. I was at peace. I was ready for the "blood blaster."

Half an hour passed and I began to feel better. My vital signs were stabilizing and I was breathing with assistance. My cell phone, tucked under my side all this time, rang. It was Mel. He was calm but scared. "Don't talk, just listen." he said. He said he had already talked with the doctor and knew I had suffered a heart attack. He had called my children, my brother, Joe, and my sister, Diane. They were all on their way. Mel would be arriving soon. "I love you." he said and hung up. It occurred to me that I might never see him again.

Things had finally quieted down. I was alone again and thinking about my life. The nurse returned to talk with me. She had heard about Aimee from the paramedics. She had called the hotel to check on Aimee, knowing I would be concerned. She wanted to personally reassure me that Aimee was fine. Aimee was with Mike at the front desk where the hotel staff were providing her care, the nurse said. She had breakfast and was playing on a computer and entertaining the staff with her funny comments. Relieved at hearing this, at least for the moment,

I knew she would be fine. Aimee always knew how to make the best of every situation.

My phone rang again. It was my friend Mario. Mel had called him and he could not believe I'd had a heart attack. "Matsu," he said, "what happened to you?" He wanted to know if the ER doctor had confirmed that it was a heart attack. I explained what had happened. As a physician and friend, he knew I was very health conscious. He knew I had never been ill with anything serious in my life. I wasn't overweight, didn't have high blood pressure, didn't have particularly high cholesterol, was not diabetic or out of shape. But I did have heart disease in my family history. Two of my mother's brothers died in their early forties from heart attacks.

The ER doctor concluded that since I didn't appear to have other symptoms, my biggest risk factor was family history. I shared this information with Mario. "But you've never had any symptoms!" he insisted. I've subsequently learned that women have completely different symptoms from men, often seemingly unrelated to what might be perceived as a heart attack. I was so naïve; I foolishly thought a heart attack was the Hollywood type with severe chest pain, falling to the floor, and gasping for air! In reality, a heart attack usually presents itself in a completely different way, especially for women.

My cell phone rang again. This time it was my sister's husband, John. He wanted to know if I was okay. He also wanted me to know that my sister was making flight arrangements to come as soon as possible. The nurse saw me on the phone and immediately reprimanded me, "What in the world are you doing with that cell phone?" She continued, "Put it away right now; you've just had a major heart attack and should be resting, not talking on the phone!" She stood there until I hung up and immediately took the phone from me and put it in my purse under the gurney. I was pleased that my sister would be arriving soon. She would take care of Aimee.

Now stable, after three hours in the ER, I was transferred to the ICU where I would remain, awaiting a cardiac evaluation later that day. I was scared, really scared. I lay there and continued to think about my life.

. . .

I recalled my favorite memories and images of growing up with cousins and family, my father and his fantastic workshop that I loved to explore as a child, and my mother and the truly exceptional and loving home she created for her children. I thought about my children then and now. I mulled over the challenges of parenthood and wondered if I'd done all the right things. I thought about the grandchildren and, in particular, I thought about Aimee and what she meant to me.

I thought about cherished friendships and all the places in the world I'd had the good fortune to see. I contemplated the successes and failures of my life and wondered about my future, and whether I would continue to have one. Would I ever travel to Italy again to see my relatives? I reflected on twenty years of happy marriage and the many experiences I had shared with Mel.

Blessed with loving parents from birth, I had continued to be blessed throughout my life. Not wealthy, but with devoted family and friends who loved me. If it was my time I was ready. If I pulled through this I would forever be grateful for the opportunity to fulfill my dreams. I would make every day count. I would finish my book.

. . .

I was jolted out of my reverie by a man who approached my bed. He was small in stature, dark skinned, beautifully dressed, and sported a long, braided beard that appeared to be tucked under his turban. I realized that he was introducing himself as my cardiologist.

He explained that I had suffered a serious heart attack and that an angiogram was necessary as soon as possible to identify and determine the extent of cardiac damage. I listened carefully when he told me that bypass surgery would follow immediately, if necessary. This was a reality check! I wasn't going anywhere, least of all home to San Jose, where I could see doctors I knew. After hearing what he had to say, I asked that no surgery be performed until my family arrived and, preferably, not until I had time to think about it. I agreed to the angiogram that afternoon. He said he would give me every consideration of time until my family arrived if I required surgery.

I worried about Aimee and wondered how she was. I returned to reminiscing about my life and soon dozed off. The phone woke me when Mel called to say he had arrived at the hotel to check on Aimee. She was fine and would remain with staff until my sister Diane arrived later that afternoon. Mel told me that Aimee asked about me and said she was "scared and sad" and missed me but, nevertheless, was having a good time with the staff. I was extremely grateful for their help and grateful for Mel's encouragement and support. Under that façade though, I knew he was frightened and trying not to show it. I explained what I knew about my situation and was comforted when he said he would follow up with the doctor.

It was time for the angiogram and I was really frightened when I was taken to the heart lab, where the procedure would be performed under local anesthetic. I watched on the monitor. Then, suddenly, everything came to an abrupt halt and the physician left the room. I intuitively knew it was a bad sign. I began asking what happened but I only received empty glances in response. I feared the worst. The cardiologist returned shortly and informed me that surgery would be necessary. In keeping with my wishes, and against his advice, it was scheduled for the following day on April 1, April Fool's Day.

My family arrived by late afternoon. Diane took a cab from the airport directly to the hotel where she took over Aimee's care. Jason drove from Modesto. My brother and his wife drove from Sacramento and picked up my daughter Janna on the way. I was grateful for their love and support, for their presence at my side.

• • •

Meanwhile, at the hotel, Aimee repeatedly asked about me. She wanted to know where I was and she wanted to see me. She was quite concerned about what happened to me and, I'm sure, understood that I would never have left her unless it was serious. Diane and Jason brought her to the hospital to see me. She was not allowed in the room but had to remain at the nurse's station looking in. Learning that Aimee couldn't see me from that distance, the nurse relented and allowed her in the room for a few minutes. I couldn't sit up, but I held her hand and reassured her that I was all right. I told her I loved her and was proud of her for helping me that morning by being such a mature girl. She smiled and told me she had fun at the hotel with Mike and the others.

• • •

The surgery was a success. I remained in intensive care for six days and was transferred to a cardiac care unit, where I remained for two more days. Eight days in the hospital was enough for me. I was eager to go home.

Jason and Aimee made the return trip to Modesto by car. I deeply regretted the premature termination of her therapy. Before they left, Aimee visited me again. I could hardly move but managed to hold her hand as Jason lifted her to the side of the bed. She needed to know that I was okay. Seeing me and talking with me in person gave her that reassurance. I wanted to see her, too, and was relieved that she was not scared when she saw me.

Mel and Janna remained in Anaheim with me until I was discharged from the hospital. The doctors would not allow me to fly, not even for one hour. The surgeon said it was too risky, and I was therefore offered two options. One was to stay in Anaheim for two or three weeks until my doctors released me to fly. The other was to make the trip to San Jose by car over a two-day period.

Neither choice was appealing, but I opted for the drive. We drove to Santa Barbara the first day. Bored, and tired of being indoors, we took a short driving tour through Solvang, where we enjoyed the warm sun and an ice cream cone. I was worn out and fatigued from the ride but felt better after a short nap and a hot meal. The second day's journey was better. I sat in the backseat where I could stretch out, enjoyed the scenery along Highway 101, and talked on my cell phone for hours. I had a lot of catching up to do. I was relieved when we arrived home.

• • •

Aimee continued to ask about me and to express her concern. Jason and Janise brought her to see me one week after I returned home. She had lots of questions that she asked over and over. "Grammy, are you okay?" she asked. "Did you have surgery? Do you still have your heart attack?" "I love you, I'm so happy to see you!" "I wanted to see you, Grammy, I wanted to see you!"

I enjoyed that visit so much. I was equally concerned about her and was very happy to see her again. I didn't want this incident to traumatize her in any way and it appeared as though it had not. I wanted to be absolutely sure that she knew I left her only because I had no other choice. I was grateful for her trust in me in a moment of crisis. I was especially happy to be alive for Aimee's sake and was already thinking about the next therapy session so we could make up for lost time.

Janna remained in San Jose for the next four weeks to assist me during the initial recovery period. She went home to Orangevale on the weekends. Her help was incredible—she planned meals, shopped, cooked, and cared for me. Mel and I couldn't have managed without her. We also had time for some lengthy discussion about the store. Janna had been commuting from Northern California to San Jose every week to work in the store. She had been staying at our house for three to four days a week so that she could work and not have a long drive every day. After serious consideration, we agreed to close the retail operation, temporarily at first; later, we decided to close it permanently. Commuting was taking its toll on Janna and although we immensely enjoyed working together, she really wanted to be closer to her home and husband. I understood and encouraged her to do what was best for her. As soon as I was able, I would continue to do design work by appointment from my home office. This decision was a relief for us both, and we felt it was the right thing to do.

• • •

Aimee was clearly a driving force in my recovery. I was given the gift of life and I intended to make good on it by picking up where I had left off. My initial recovery period went well, and I did everything by the book. I joined a cardiac rehabilitation group at a local hospital and ate a heart-healthy diet. Then I had a setback, a complication that required medication, which resulted in terrible side effects. I had to get beyond it and knew I had to get well or I could not continue to help Aimee.

My primary goal was to regain my health and strength. Without that, I knew my family would lose confidence in my ability to care for Aimee on another month-long therapy trip. Aimee gave me purpose, provided direction and a reason to live. She, more than anyone else, was counting on me for a full recovery.

• • •

Aimee had helped others recover also. Janise told me a story about Aimee's school bus driver, who after two years had unexpectedly stopped driving the bus. She was gone for about six months. Aimee liked this woman very much and waited for Kathy to arrive each morning to drive her to school. When a new and different driver appeared, Aimee told her mother several times that Kathy was "sick" but provided no other information. No one knew what had happened to her. Then, early one morning while preparing for school, Aimee shocked Janise by telling her that the bus was coming and that Kathy was driving it. Astounded by this comment because it was so odd and unexpected, she was even more amazed when the bus turned the corner and there was Kathy behind the wheel!

Kathy arrived early so she could explain to Janise how happy she was that she could return to work. She said that Aimee was responsible for saving her life. She said that she had become depressed and attempted suicide. She hadn't wanted to live. Then, during her hospitalization, she remembered Aimee and her big smile each day, and how Aimee always told her that she liked her. Aimee's positive attitude and friendly, loving spirit inspired her to appreciate her life. She said that she had used Aimee's image as part of her daily recovery plan and that Aimee's words gave her strength and a new desire to live. If Aimee could be so happy in her life with all that she had going against her, then Kathy thought she had a responsibility to make her life count because she had so much more. Because of Aimee, she had pulled through. It was a beautiful story.

• • •

As time passed Aimee's preoccupation with my surgery and health diminished. For this I was grateful. Then, months later, while visiting us one weekend, she brought it up again. As is our typical Sunday morning routine, we had coffee and read the newspaper in bed. In the morning, Mel carried her into our room where she sat in the middle of our bed while we talked and giggled. Then Mel left the room to take a shower and Aimee and I were alone. Soon she said, "Grammy, can I ask you a question?"

"Yes," I replied, "You can ask me anything you want." Then, with concern in her voice she asked, "Grammy, do you still have your heart attack?" I reassured her that I no longer had a heart attack and that I was all better now. Then I asked her if she remembered when I went to the hospital and had my surgery. She did and said that she had been "scared, very scared." Surprised with her response, I wanted to find out how much she actually understood and if she recalled the paramedics bursting into the room and carrying me away. I asked, "Do you remember who took me to the hospital?"

Her response stunned me. "Oh yes, Grammy, I remember," she said. "I remember I saw her, I saw her go with you to the hospital."

Confused now and wondering what she was talking about, I asked again, "Aimee, who did you see go to the hospital with me? The firemen took me to the hospital, do you remember?" She responded again, this time very serious and direct. "No, no, no! No, Grammy, no! Nuna took you to the hospital. I saw her and she went with you! She went with you to the hospital."

I was shaken by her response. I was prompting her to remember the paramedics and how they helped. But she was talking about my mother, "Nuna" to her, who had died four years earlier. She was adamant and insisted several times that Nuna went with me. I didn't argue.

Then, to my surprise, she said, "I want to say a prayer for Nuna." Holding her twisted little hands together in prayer, she said, "Dear God, take care of Nuna. Amen." I was so touched by her astounding display of spirituality that I was left speechless. I hugged her and wiped the tears from my eyes.

When I told Mel, he recalled another incident earlier in the weekend. While he was holding Aimee on his lap, she kept looking over his shoulder and straining her head to look around him in the opposite direction. Annoyed, he asked her what she was doing and what she was looking at. She told him, "I'm looking over there. I see her over there by the door. She's there, right by the door." Mel didn't understand. Then she said, "Tutu, don't you see her over there? It's Nuna and she is standing right there!" When he recounted this to me, we both had goose bumps and wondered why Aimee would say such a thing. She was only three when my mother died, but she had not forgotten the dear woman who loved her so much.

• • •

This wasn't the first time, or the last, that Aimee made such comments about people who were dead. She had done it many times before. Aimee mentions them as if they are present. One day she began talking to Janise about a person named "Zamora." Surprised, Janise asked, "Why are you saying that, Aimee?" She was positive Aimee did not know her maiden name. She was curious and spooked that Aimee should mention it. Then Aimee exclaimed, "I see Zamora in the room." Janise's grandfather and an Uncle Zamora had both been dead for a number of years long before Aimee's birth. What was she seeing so clearly that we could not?

NEW MOBILITY

MONTHS WOULD HAVE TO PASS before I would be well enough to take Aimee to therapy again, but I was determined to do so. Although my overall recovery went well, I suffered painful complications of pericarditis, inflammation of the membrane encasing the heart. This condition required special medication and I had to stay close to home. I had several clients who were waiting patiently for my services, and I was eager to return to work. I began to focus my efforts on two intertwined goals: to take charge and direct my own recovery program so I could get back to work and to take Aimee to therapy again.

I was concerned about Aimee. She had already missed two therapy sessions, victim of the unfortunate consequences of her hip surgery and my heart attack. I feared missing three consecutive sessions would result in a deterioration of her condition. I realized that I was the only person in Aimee's life who, at this time, could make these therapy sessions available to her. If I didn't take her, nobody would.

To accomplish my first goal, I took my doctor's advice and enrolled in the cardiac rehabilitation program at O'Connor Hospital in San Jose. During my recovery, I was forbidden to lift anything more than a few pounds. In reality, I was too weak to lift anything, and I knew I couldn't lift Aimee again until I developed the body strength to do so. It would be a long road, but I was confident the cardiac workouts would help me accomplish this task. The program consisted of exercise, stress management, and nutrition classes. I signed up for the early morning class, three mornings a week. This wasn't easy for me. I have never enjoyed working out and, other than formal ballet classes for a number of years in my thirties, I had never had a regular or structured exercise regime. I had done early morning walks with the dog, but that had been sporadic at best.

My commitment kept me focused. Caring for Aimee required lifting her—in and out of bed, her chair, the tub, and the car. I would also have to lift and carry her equipment. If I ever planned to take her to therapy again, I knew I needed to work even harder.

One day on the treadmill at my cardiac rehabilitation class, my heart felt a little odd. It began racing faster and faster. Assuming at first that it was a normal increase in heart rate, it didn't take long to realize that it was beating out of control. Luckily, I was being monitored at the time and the nurse also observed the increase. I was immediately removed from the treadmill and placed in a chair. We waited. My doctor was contacted when it continued to pound, reaching a level of over 250 beats per minute.

I was quickly admitted to the hospital and scheduled for a cardioversion procedure, which consisted of receiving a general anesthetic, after which they stopped and restarted my heart with a paddle defibrillator. Once the process was completed, I was awakened and released after two hours in recovery. To my disappointment, I was placed back on the very medication I hated to take. It would regulate my heart, but the side effects, not the least of which was weight gain, were unpleasant and uncomfortable. This was a setback for me, but it made me all the more determined to work even harder.

The school year was coming to a close. I usually planned activities with the grandchildren during summer vacation, but I couldn't do it this year. Aimee, unlike her siblings who had many invitations and activities planned for their summer vacation, had little to do. Other than summer school for a few weeks, summer vacations were long and boring for her.

Earlier in the year, before my heart attack, we had planned a family river-rafting trip to Northern California in July, with Janna and her husband, Greg. We were planning to tow my vintage Airstream trailer there for a fun weekend away from the city. I convinced my family that we should go and suggested we take Chloe along for the weekend. She could manage herself and was well behaved. We had a great time and I enjoyed time to relax and float down the river.

But Mel felt a longer vacation was in order. He needed a rest, and we needed some time to get away. My physician discouraged air travel but said I was free to travel anywhere by car. We decided to take a ten-day vacation to Oregon in late August. We could drive and the timing was perfect. I was delighted when Mel suggested we take Aimee along. He would do the lifting; I would do the dressing and feeding. We would share the other tasks. Her summer had been uneventful and we knew she would enjoy this time with us. Aimee was excited and told everyone she talked to that she was going on vacation to Oregon with us.

We picked her up in Modesto on our way to Lake Shasta, where we spent our first night. From there we traveled north to Ashland, Oregon. As we drove further north along the Oregon coastline, Aimee repeatedly asked to "stop by the beach." We didn't know how she knew we were driving along the coast, because we didn't think she could see it, especially from her seat by the opposite window. We assumed then that she could smell the sea air and when I asked her, she responded with "I can smell the ocean!"

This reminded me of our times in Anaheim when her heightened sense of smell became apparent early on, as did her sensitivity to noise. I particularly noticed this in Anaheim when we went for a walk. If we headed toward Downtown Disney, she knew it because she could smell the Peruvian lilies bordering the avenue. If we walked in the opposite direction, toward the therapy center, she smelled the jasmine and knew exactly where we were going. I would pick flowers for her to hold and smell.

"What does it mean to smell, Grammy?" She would ask. Often she would ask me the name of a flower, "Grammy, what is that flower? I smell a new flower." These questions and comments gave me with insight into Aimee's world. Like all children her age, she was curious and asked simple questions to help her understand and learn about the world around her.

. . .

While in Oregon, we were caught in an awful storm, which made it impossible to stop at any of the beaches. We continued on to Portland, where we remained for a few days to see the local sights, and then we went on to Mt. Hood, where we had reservations at the beautiful and rustic Timberland Lodge. Our next stop was the stunning Crater Lake, where we were fortunate to stay at another historic lodge before returning home. The trip was wonderful in spite of the rain and unusually cold temperatures. Predictably, Aimee was excellent in every way. Hikes and sightseeing became our routine and Aimee enjoyed it all.

While in Portland, we walked from our hotel along the waterfront one evening to eat dinner at a seafood restaurant on the pier. It began to rain, and then it stormed as we rushed back to the warmth of our hotel after dinner. We covered Aimee with our coats to keep her dry, but we got soaked from running against the rain. At our hotel room, as we dried off and began to settle down, I reached for my cell phone to make a call. I couldn't find it. I was sure I had had it with me at the restaurant and thought perhaps I had left it there. We called the restaurant; they searched and did not find it. We tore our room apart looking for it. We looked everywhere and even called the phone several times just in case it was there. Nothing. Finally, I insisted on walking back to the restaurant and checking carefully along the promenade where we had walked earlier. Perhaps it had fallen out of my coat pocket and someone had found it. Mel remained with Aimee. Cold and storming, I was breathless by the time I reached the restaurant. I checked everywhere and still no phone. On my return, I stopped at every shop along the way to ask if anyone had found a phone. No phone.

Meanwhile, back at the hotel, Aimee kept telling Mel that she knew where the phone was. He had called it several times, thinking he might hear it ringing in the hallway or some obscure place. No success; he didn't hear a thing. Aimee kept insisting it was "over there" or "in there" but when he looked, there was nothing. She continued to insist, "Tutu, look over there!" His searches again turned up nothing. Finally, frustrated, having exhausted all options except one, he decided to roll Aimee around the room and listen to what she had to say. When they approached my suitcase, she said it was there. Sure enough, when Mel opened my suitcase again and tilted it on its side and shook it, the phone fell out. It had apparently dropped out of my pocket and into the folded garment section, hidden from view.

Aimee's hearing is so acute that she heard what we could not. She was pleased that Mel found the phone and insisted that he call me with it. He had to explain to her that they couldn't call me because they had my phone. He assured her that I would be very happy when I returned. They called the restaurant hoping to find me so I could conclude my search, but I had already left. Later, when I returned, cold and discouraged, I was revitalized when they showed me the phone. Aimee was so excited and couldn't wait to tell me how they found it. She was proud of herself when I praised her for being a "hero" for finding my phone. Years later, this event is still fresh in her mind and we still laugh at the situation whenever she mentions it to us.

. . .

Rested, we returned home and quickly fell back into our normal activities. Aimee returned to school, Mel to work, and I to cardiac rehabilitation. I felt better, was getting stronger, and was confident I could manage Aimee by myself in a few months. Failing to reach my goal wasn't an option. I had observed Aimee slouching in her chair, head dropping a little, and arms tightening by her sides. I knew the positive effects of the previous therapy sessions were wearing off. As she grew, the gains made in the past were slowly diminishing, and I wanted to help her regain the strength she had before she lost it all.

I knew Poland would be out of the question, so I began to inquire about availability at the Anaheim center. There was an opening available for the March 2005 session, so I signed us up. I also made our reservations at the same Residence Inn. The staff were pleased to hear that we would be returning and looked forward to seeing us again.

Now, I just had to convince Jason and Janise that I could do it. I hadn't discussed it with them until I was sure there was an opening. Mel stood behind me on this and provided encouragement all the way. He knew better than to try to discourage me once my mind was made up.

The year finally came to a close and I was doing much better by then and feeling strong. I was pleased with myself for having successfully achieved my goal. I felt confident about handling Aimee alone and prepared for the trip with enthusiasm. To my surprise, my son and daughter-in-law were pleased that Aimee's therapy would resume and that I wanted to take her again. I was sure they also would welcome a break from her day-to-day care; it had been a long time since they had had one.

• • •

Janna remained most concerned. She openly expressed her doubts regarding our safety, especially making the long drive alone with Aimee. To solve this problem, I invited her to join us on our trip to Southern California. To her delight, I planned a leisurely journey south. We took pleasure in visiting several of the historical California missions along the route and spent two days in scenic Santa Barbara. Janna embraced the chance to spend quality time with Aimee, and they clearly enjoyed being together. Janna was amused, if somewhat bewildered, by Aimee's ability to converse continually about anything and everything. Having experienced this phenomenon in the past, I quietly drew pleasure from listening to them as I drove. We didn't rush and were rested when we arrived at our hotel three days later.

We were greeted at the hotel with an unexpected change. They were in the process of renovating guest rooms. Our familiar and comfortable suite had been recently redecorated and was ready for us to occupy. We opened the door to the smell of fresh paint, bright wallpaper, new carpet, and attractive new furnishings. I was elated by the kindness and consideration the hotel staff extended in making our stay comfortable and pleasant.

Janna was a tremendous help. She had packed up the room a year earlier when I'd had my heart attack and drew from that experience to help me unpack and arrange our things now. She stayed with Aimee while I shopped for groceries.

A relatively simple task for most people, shopping for groceries requires a strategy when you're alone with Aimee in tow. Incapable of sitting in a grocery cart, she must remain in her wheelchair or stroller. If only a few items are needed they can be carried in a basket, but a cart is required if you are shopping for several days, or in our case, for the month. Pushing a cart and a wheelchair at the same time is difficult to manage. I've learned that I can push Aimee in front of me in her chair and pull the cart behind me as I navigate store aisles. It is a slow but effective way to complete the task. Janna's offer to watch Aimee while I shopped simplified the process considerably. I was able to quickly complete my grocery shopping and return to the hotel.

Once, while at a Trader Joe's store in Glendale, Aimee and I began shopping as I described. The store manager quickly approached and insisted on taking the shopping cart and walking along with us. He patiently waited as I read labels and made my selections. He chatted with Aimee as she bombarded him with questions and told him all about herself. I was impressed with his compassionate and caring manner. How wonderful it would be if more individuals took the initiative to help in small but important ways.

We were settled at last and Janna was ready to say good-bye. We took her to the airport the following morning. She would return at the end of the month to help pack up and accompany us on our drive home. I appreciated her help and enjoyed her companionship, too.

Aimee started her therapy the next day on March 2, 2005, and she was eager to begin. Her main therapist this time was Bret from Poland.

He was in his late twenties and Aimee adored him from the start. She often openly expressed her affection for him and made him blush. His therapy plan was to start slow while keeping things challenging for Aimee. I valued his gentle and considerate approach and the thoughtful way he related to Aimee. Her relationship with the therapist was a motivating factor, and because she was so fond of him, she worked hard to win his praise.

Mel resumed his routine of visiting us on the weekends. On his first weekend visit, he suggested we take Aimee to the Huntington Museum in Pasadena. Aimee waited in great anticipation to see the paintings of "Blue Boy" and "Pinky" that Mel had told her about. Aimee couldn't get enough museum time to satisfy her curiosity. At her insistence, we wheeled her from painting to painting, room to room, exhibit to exhibit. She delighted in the experience and when asked about her favorite paintings she loudly proclaimed, "Pinky is my favorite!" Indeed, she carried the brochure from the museum with a picture of the little girl, "Pinky" for days, clutching it tightly in her hands. We promised we would take her again soon.

One day at the center, Maggie, a senior therapist, approached me to talk about a walker for Aimee. She had recently treated a boy with similar physical limitations and thought a walker like his would benefit Aimee. Soon after, a representative from the company that made the walkers contacted me to arrange a meeting. He wanted to meet Aimee and observe her during therapy. He agreed to bring a walker for Aimee to try and explained the complexities of adjusting it to her size. A few days later, he arrived with the walker, measured Aimee, and watched her therapy. Then he adjusted the walker and prepared it for a trial run.

The contraption consisted of three separate parts: the base, the stanchion, and the body brace. The first part, the base, could be adapted with two, three, or four wheels in various configurations, depending on the child's balance. Aimee would start with four wheels, two in front and two in back. Eventually, this could progress to only one wheel in front or in back. The stanchion locked into a notch in the base.

Adjusted to accommodate Aimee's height, it would receive and hold the body brace. The third and most complex section, the body brace, was strapped onto Aimee, starting at the feet. Special high-topped shoes slipped into locks on each side of the ankle braces when connected with the jointed knee and hip straps. The bilateral steel braces connected to a bar that held the torso rigid, with loosely fitting straps around her waist and upper torso. Fitted in the body brace, Aimee was then lifted by holding the side of the body brace and placed onto the stanchion, where a notch in the back locked her in place. All three parts, working together, would provide body support for Aimee to stand upright so that she could then take steps and move forward.

The representative said that it often took days, if not weeks, for a child to actually move in the walker, because of the unfamiliar feeling of standing upright and having mobility. When he clicked Aimee into place, she startled at the noise and, frightened, began to cry. But she quickly regained control when she realized she would not fall. With my encouragement, she began to step forward and then started walking in the walker! We were amazed. Parents lined up to watch her as she squealed and screamed with joy and said, "I'm walking, look at me Grammy look at me! Are you watching me?" Every parent was in tears. Hands over my face in awe, I laughed and cried simultaneously at her enthusiasm. Soon she wanted to "race" with everyone. "Let's race," she said to Bret, as he helped her out the door. Then she wanted to "cross the street" to the other side of the parking lot. She walked in this fashion for approximately thirty minutes until she was exhausted and could only take a few steps and stop. Aimee had shocked me in the past at what she could do, but I was stunned at her ability to move so fast. Therapy and walking in the Adeli suit had paid off. She had the movements down pat. I was so thrilled for her and to see her so happy.

At my request, the sales representative agreed to leave the walker with us for five days over the long Easter weekend. Mel was coming and I was eager for him to see Aimee and to hear his opinion. Getting her in and out of the brace was somewhat complicated and difficult. I showed Mel how it worked, and once he understood he was able to help. We agreed that Aimee should have the walker, but the price of almost $6,000 was prohibitive and an important consideration. We had to research it more.

During a previous Anaheim session, we had met a wonderful family from Laguna Beach. June heard we were there and invited us to spend Easter Sunday at their home. Her little girl, Alexa, was younger than Aimee and also had cerebral palsy. June was devoted to helping her child and provided her with every possible therapy and equipment. She had become close friends with one of the former Polish therapists from the center and had invited her to share in the Easter celebration as well. June urged us to bring the walker so she could see how it worked. When we arrived at their home we were surprised to see Bret, Aimee's therapist. June had also invited him so he would not spend the holiday alone.

After enjoying a delicious meal and Easter egg hunt with the children, we put the girls in their walkers. Alexa was in her smaller, less complex walker and Aimee in her trial walker. Aimee took off immediately, almost running out of control and showing off for Bret. He stayed with her and was encouraged by her body movement and control. Mel followed behind with the video camera while Jane and I watched. It was great fun for Aimee; she loved the attention.

Later June showed me an adaptive "bike" (a tricycle) they had bought for Alexa. It was too big for their daughter and was stored in the garage. She thought maybe Aimee could try it. Aimee had never been on a bicycle or tricycle, and I was doubtful that she would know what to do or even how to pedal. But if she didn't get scared, we could definitely give it a try. Aimee was having the time of her life in the walker and eager to try something new, especially the tricycle.

We strapped her in the seat, strapped her feet in the pedals and away she went! She took off so fast that Bret had to run after her to catch her before she headed straight down the sloping driveway and into the street. At the bottom of the driveway she managed to pedal herself back up to the top, only to ride down again and again. She didn't want to get off and was totally thrilled by her newfound sport.

On our way home, Mel and I discussed how we might purchase a tricycle for Aimee. We agreed that, no matter what, she had to have one. We understood the cost was approximately $2,500 but thought we could manage it somehow.

We were very excited about Aimee's accomplishments in the walker and called Jason and Janise with the news. They were quite interested and wanted to see the video clip of Aimee in action. We had footage to show them when we returned home. Of course, the main consideration was the price of almost $6,000. Janise agreed to inquire with their insurance company regarding benefits for equipment. Even so, they would have to pay at least half.

We would have to figure out something else for the trike. It was definitely not covered by insurance.

• • •

It stormed the following weekend, but Mel arrived with a smile. He was happy to see us. Because of the predicted rainfall all weekend I made arrangements for us to go to the Norton-Simon Museum in Los Angeles to see a French impressionist exhibit. One of the family activities at the museum that Saturday was for children to make a *chapeau*, a hat. I thought Aimee would enjoy the museum.

Aimee was just like other children, pushing to be at the front of the table, selecting her materials for her hat. She required assistance to cut, paste, and color but worked on her hat until she was satisfied with the results. She was proud of her hat and, when finished, took great pleasure in wearing it the entire day while touring the exhibit halls.

We stopped for lunch at the museum restaurant and then toured more exhibits until late afternoon. Of course, Aimee wanted to see every piece of art in every room. She would say, "Scoot me closer, scoot me closer, please!" until she was rolled to exactly where she wanted to be so that she could see. Aimee's good manners took many adults by surprise when they would turn to see a little girl in a wheelchair speaking to them.

• • •

That evening we dined at a favorite restaurant near our hotel. As we had done in the past, we sat on the terrace to accommodate Aimee's wheelchair and not inconvenience other patrons. While waiting for our entrees, we noticed the pleasant piano music playing in the background. Actually, the speaker was mounted on the wall above and behind Aimee's head. While Mel and I talked, she listened to the music and exclaimed with a great sigh, "Oh, I'm in heaven listening to this piano music!" We were amused by her comment and chuckled to ourselves. When the server returned, she told him the same thing, so I asked if he could please find out the name of the artist or the CD that was playing.

Aimee interrupted, insisting that it wasn't a CD but a man playing the piano. When we disagreed, she became emphatic. "No, no no! It's a man playing the piano!" she repeated. The waiter told her that he was sorry, but he was positive it was a CD. When he left, I assured her that we would find out about the CD and I would try to buy it for her if she liked it so much. She insisted again that it was not a CD and became argumentative with me when I disagreed. "No, Grammy, it's a man in the other room—a man who is playing the piano, in there, in the other room!" Her insistence and persistence were beginning to annoy us, because we were certain the music was coming from the speaker above her head and that was why it sounded so real.

Soon the server returned, smiling but humble as he apologized to Aimee. He said that he hadn't known it earlier because it was, indeed unusual, but there was a man playing the piano in the bar! Of course, Aimee wanted to see for herself. The next thing I knew, we were working our way through the crowded restaurant to the cocktail lounge. There he was, a man playing a white piano. Aimee wanted to be up close and personal. I allowed her to listen to one song only and then I had to insist that we return to our table. After all, it was a bar and not appropriate for a little girl. Aimee was satisfied and gloated as she told Mel all about the "piano man."

• • •

It had been another successful month. We had both done well. Best of all, Aimee had discovered two new means of mobility that she could enjoy. This was an enormous milestone for her. Being able to move about with others, and in the company of her family, would have a huge impact on her life. I was satisfied with Aimee's progress in therapy and with her schoolwork, too. Her teacher had sent a month's worth of classroom assignments, which we completed daily. I regretted that Aimee missed school but did my best to help her maintain her studies and homework.

Janna returned on the last day of the session and joined us at the center. It was March 30, a year to the date when I had suffered my heart attack at the same hotel. It felt good to have made it through the entire month without incident and on my own. I was proud of myself and of Aimee. We packed up our car and prepared to head home.

We left very early the next morning to avoid commuter traffic through Los Angeles. I drove, Aimee talked, and Janna listened. In the past, I've shared many stories with Aimee about my father, her great-grand-father, and how as a young boy he traveled from Italy to America. She repeated the entire story to Janna. When finished, she asked questions about every family member she could think of. What impressed me the most during this exchange was her ability to remember names, places, and details. She entertained us for hours.

• • •

When we showed Jason and Janise the video clip of Aimee in the walker and on the tricycle, they were stunned. They watched in disbelief at Aimee's efforts to master these two new pieces of equipment. Her enthusiasm burst forth from the screen. Aimee is often left out of many fun family activities with her siblings because she cannot participate. Seeing the video now, it was difficult not to be excited for her. Mel and I wanted to give her anything that would bring her happiness and help her to be the best she could be. The trike would certainly bring her new opportunities to develop her physical stamina and social interaction skills with other kids.

Ordering a walker would take months. First, Janise would have to apply and go through a complicated insurance authorization process. The walker would then have to be ordered from Europe, where it was manufactured. The special shoes had to be ordered from Denmark and would have to be fitted with hardware. The trike, on the other hand, was readily available. I wasn't about to let the opportunity pass for Aimee to enjoy her newfound mobility. I was on a mission to get her trike as quickly as I could. She deserved that and more. Equipped with a brochure and information, I planned to make contact with the representative to place an order as soon as possible.

I succeeded in locating the regional representative and arranged for him to meet us at our home the following Sunday morning. This would give Jason and Janise time to make arrangements to join us. The rep brought the model I had requested so that Aimee's parents could see her in action. The device has three wheels and is larger than a standard tricycle and smaller than an adult style tricycle that you often see seniors riding. When the handlebars are locked, an adult can manipulate the steering and control the tricycle from a bar located behind the child's seat. This requires that an adult walk or run next to it or behind it. The same option applies to the braking system.

In Aimee's case, because she could not steer or brake with her own hands, an adult would do it for her. The large adaptive seat with back support and a butterfly harness held her tight against the seat. There was a lap strap if needed and her feet were strapped onto the foot pedals and held in place with Velcro straps.

Jason and Janise arrived with Aimee as planned. She knew exactly why she was there and could hardly wait to ride the trike again. More important, she could hardly wait to show her father what she could do. It was one of those moments when Aimee's joy was contagious. I was secretly pleased that they felt it was important enough to bring Aimee back to San Jose for the purpose of trying out a tricycle. I could hardly wait to see her ride.

She immediately made friends with the sales representative as he measured and fitted her to the trike. "Hi, Derick, what are you doing now?" she asked. "Is this my bicycle?" Her feet were already pushing forward and he had to hold her back as he made the adjustments for her size. She quickly learned how to apply the brakes with her feet and was rocking the trike back and forth. She wanted to "race" and couldn't wait to take off. As soon as his hands came off the tricycle she took off down the street with all of us chasing her! Remember, Aimee cannot see well and could not see where she was going. She was on the sidewalk but veering toward the curb, which could result in serious injury if she fell.

"Let's race, Daddy!" she yelled. "Try to catch me!" Jason ran fast and managed to grab her, laughing as he breathed heavily from the effort. She wanted to ride up and down the block, which she did until she tired us out, one by one. Curious, neighbors came out to see the tricycle and Aimee in action. She loved the attention as they cheered and clapped when she returned to the starting point. Once, as she took off with Mel, Jason turned to me and said, "Mom, this is fantastic. Now we can take Aimee to the park with the other kids and she can ride her trike, too. Choked with emotion, he continued, "It's going to be a wonderful family activity that we can all do together. This is going to make such a big difference for Aimee and our family."

My heart swelled with joy for everyone but especially for Aimee. For her, it was like Christmas morning, an experience she never really shares in as fully as the other children. That morning, though, was Aimee's Christmas in my eyes. She was ecstatic and her heartfelt smile, sparkling eyes, and shouts of joy said it all. Merry Christmas, Aimee!

So Aimee would have her own "bicycle." We ordered it that morning and it would be one size larger to accommodate her growth. She remained with us overnight so that on Monday she could be fitted for her own new blue bicycle.

She exhausted me that Monday morning, running up and down the street with her. And she kept telling me what to do. "Cross the street, I want to go across the street now!" She demanded. She was bossy and wanted to see Jack, our neighbor. "I want to go to Jack's house; I want to go there right now!" Another admirer, Jack, offered to take her down the block. He didn't know what he was getting himself into until he returned exhausted and out of breath. I literally had to pull Aimee off the trike that day when her legs began shaking with muscle spasms. I had to insist it was time to stop and go inside. I was tired. After lunch I drove a very happy little girl and her blue bicycle home to Modesto.

THE WHEELCHAIR GIRL

CHAPTER 17

AIMEE'S SELF-ESTEEM BLOSSOMED as her speech development, cognitive abilities, and physical strength continued to improve as a result of the recent therapy sessions. And she became skilled at riding her tricycle. When she came to San Jose to visit, the trike came with her. She and her tricycle spent the weekend with us in April 2005. The weather was beautiful and we went outdoors to sit in the garden. Aimee couldn't wait to see our neighbors and said, "Grammy, I want to go outside now, I want to see Jack!" It was 7:30 a.m.

We finished with breakfast, dressed, and were ready to go out. Once Aimee was strapped on her trike, it was difficult to get her off. Rocking the pedals back and forth, ready to take off without me, she wanted to cross the street immediately. She knew where Jack lived and wanted to see him. Jack, observing from his window, came out to say hello. Aimee, delighted to see him again, shouted, "Watch me, Jack. Watch me race and go fast!" Aimee loves the attention, but Jack was not interested in running behind her down the street. He and I exchanged glances and smiles as I took off behind Aimee. He watched and waited, cheering Aimee on as we passed him, cheering me on as I struggled to keep up.

I'm not sure why Aimee continually wants to "cross the street" and "race." I believe that crossing the street must satisfy her curiosity about what's beyond her range of vision. She often says to me that she wants "to go over there," looking in a new direction, which seems to satisfy her sense of adventure for a fresh experience.

We rode, and ran, two blocks to the Rose Garden Park where Aimee could smell the roses. We needed a break; I needed a break. "Oh Grammy, I'm in heaven with my new bicycle." I knew she was happy and having a good time, and I enjoyed sharing the experience with her. She made bossy demands but I didn't care; I secretly welcomed them. Finally, two hours later, she told me her legs were tired and we went home. Aimee will probably never know, but I would take her to the ends of the earth if it meant providing her with an opportunity to have fun.

We drove to Modesto as often as possible to watch Chloe play soccer. Jason was very involved with Chloe's activities and had agreed to coach her team. He was having a successful go at it and enjoyed working with the children. Janise went to every game but seldom took Aimee with her because she cried and carried on. Startled by the sounds of clapping and cheers from the parents and spectators she didn't know, it was impossible for Aimee to relax. As disconcerting to Aimee as this was, watching her suffer was agonizing for Janise. Aimee commanded attention and unfairly took the focus away from Chloe and her game. Chloe also wanted and needed her mother's attention. Aimee therefore was usually left with a friend or babysitter for a few hours while the rest of the family went to Chloe's game.

Visits to Modesto often became a weekend affair, combining several activities with a hotel stay and meals out. On these occasions, Aimee joined us at the hotel so that the focus at home could be on Chloe and preparing for her game. This included everyone having a good night's sleep. On one weekend, I suggested to Janise that since we were there, we would bring Aimee to the game. Mel and I would take full responsibility for her and remove her if she acted up. I gave my word that we would not allow her to disrupt the game. Janise gave us her blessing.

At the hotel, and again later at the game, I quietly explained in detail to Aimee what was happening and what was expected of her if she wanted to go to the game. I used the same approach when preparing Aimee to attend any new event or activity. By now she understood the concept of demonstrating pleasure and praise through applause and had improved tremendously. She also enjoyed participating with the family, but this required that she exhibit appropriate behavior if she wanted to do so. Otherwise, she would be left at home. Although sometimes necessary, no one wants to be left at home and Aimee was no exception. I wanted to provide her with an opportunity to improve.

During a hearty breakfast, we talked about Chloe and her soccer team. "What does it mean to play soccer, Grammy?" Aimee asked. I explained that Chloe was part of a team that included other little girls. They had to play their game by the rules and their daddy was teaching the team how to do that. He was the coach. He was also teaching them how to win the game. When they ran up and down the field their parents and family clapped and yelled to encourage and support them to make a goal.

Aimee asked, "What does it mean to encourage?"

I explained that it means to cheer, to clap, and to yell for them to win the game—to inspire them. I *encouraged* her to do the same. I suggested that she could cheer for Chloe just like the other people did and that Chloe would hear her and want to do her best. I also encouraged her to cheer for her daddy to win. It would make him happy if she did that. Of course, she liked that idea a lot.

Spending long periods of time with Aimee had taught me that time invested in detailed explanations always pays off. She listened, she understood, and, when faced with an unfamiliar situation, she tried to do her best and apply what she had learned. These talks also helped teach her new words, which she absorbed and later used appropriately in her own conversations. She trusted me, and I was confident she would do fine at the game. Mel had agreed to take her to a remote section of the field if she lost control and could not tolerate the situation.

We arrived at the field early so that Aimee could familiarize herself with the surroundings while it was still relatively quiet. Mel was eager to watch Chloe in action and he shared this sentiment to get Aimee involved. He explained that it was fun to watch the game together. He took Aimee for a walk around the field and stopped to say hello to everyone she knew as they arrived. Jason and Chloe took a moment to express their pleasure that she was there. We joined Janise, Jeffrey, and the other relatives at the sidelines and set up our chairs at a safe distance from parents and spectators but still within hearing distance.

Isolating Aimee too much would defeat the purpose of integrating her and encouraging her participation. The game began. At first upset and tense, Aimee soon began to relax and cheer, "Go Chlooooooooooooeeeeeeeee!"

"Come on, Chloe, you can do it!" she yelled over and over. The clapping continued to startle her. One man kept yelling loudly and whistling. "Listen, Aimee, listen to that man. He's making all that noise so that his little girl will hear him." I continued, "Don't be scared, it's okay and you can yell and clap too."

Mel held her hands and helped her clap. She cheered and screamed when everyone else had stopped, but that didn't matter a bit because she was enjoying herself.

Chloe made two goals during the first half of the game. When she came to the sidelines, she made sure to acknowledge and say hello to Aimee every time. During halftime, Aimee was invited to have refreshments with the team. Jason and Janise praised her for being at the game and being a good girl. During the second half we took Aimee out of her chair and took turns holding her on our laps.

After a while she said to Mel, "Guess what, Tutu, guess what?"

"What?" he said

"I want to play soccer! I want to play soccer like Chloe!" Mel and I looked at each other with that all-too-familiar thought of "Poor Aimee." Reassuringly, Mel said, "Well, Aimee, maybe you can kick the ball with your feet or you can throw the ball. We can help you do that."

She thought about it a moment and, to our dismay, responded, "No, no, no. I cannot play soccer. I can't run! I'm a *wheelchair* girl, I *can't* play soccer!" Mel and I exchanged glances again, sorrow in our eyes. I had a lump in my throat and couldn't speak. I didn't know what to say, but Mel did. "That's okay, Aimee. You can do lots of other things in your wheelchair," he said encouragingly. I reminded her that even if she could not play soccer she could come to the games and cheer for Chloe.

Despite our reassurances, Aimee's profound comment hit home. It was a depressing moment. She was getting older and undoubtedly becoming increasingly aware of her own limitations. I knew what Aimee's boundaries were, but now it was obvious that she knew what they were, too. Nevertheless we would continue to help her in her quest to "run and play" along with the other kids in whatever way possible.

• • •

Janise received notices regularly inviting Aimee to participate in "adaptive" sports activities such as snow skiing and water skiing. "Water skiing—how could she do that?" I asked. Janise explained. We discussed the possibility several times and thought Aimee would enjoy water skiing because she took pleasure, most of the time, in water activities—especially the swimming pool. Janise asked me if we would be willing to take Aimee. I told her of course we would.

When the day came, we had to be in Modesto at 6:30 a.m. to pick up Aimee. From there we would drive to a nearby lake. At the last moment, Janise changed her mind and decided that she, Jeffrey, and Chloe would join us. It was going to be a hot day and the other kids would enjoy the lake too. Terrific, I thought, it would be a fun day for everyone. I made sandwiches and snacks and packed the picnic basket. Mel loaded the ice chest and we were on our way to Modesto. The lake was desolate: no trees, dry grass, an arid landscape. The environment was unpleasant and unappealing to me, but Aimee was excited and that's what counted. I explained everything to the best of my knowledge in detail to her. Most of all, I said she would have lots of fun with the other kids. They would all take turns being pulled behind the boat, splashing and going fast in the water. She liked the idea of going fast.

We drove around the lake looking for our camp. Finally we noticed a group of vans and kids in wheelchairs nestled in a small isolated cove. There were a couple of pop-up canopies to shade tables and ice chests, but no room for chairs. We didn't think to bring umbrellas with us and now would have no shade. Chloe and Jeffrey immediately ran to the water's edge while we set up our area for the day. Except for Aimee, our chairs remained unsheltered and exposed to the blazing hot sun. The day was already a scorcher, but at least we had hats.

Once settled in, I assessed the situation and began to feel uneasy. I always trust my intuition even when I don't *want* to feel what I know I am feeling. Janise seemed well informed about this group and how they were organized; even so, I asked her again if she was sure about them. She explained that two sets of parents owned the boats and that the other parents had constructed the adaptive water skis. They had done this for years. Most of the kids were older boys between the ages of ten and fourteen. There was one girl around twelve years old. Aimee was the youngest and the smallest.

I asked Janise if more kids were coming. She didn't know. This was not what I had expected, and it probably was not what Janise had envisioned. I was expecting something more organized and structured. The kids were taking turns going on the lake and undoubtedly having fun but, in my opinion, the whole setup appeared haphazard. Mel told me to stop worrying and enjoy the day. But then Mel and I checked out the ski equipment and simultaneously had the same thought. How in the world was Aimee going to do this? Mel tried to minimize his level of concern but I could see the apprehension in his eyes.

When I was much younger, I water skied often. My brother Joe had a fabulous ski boat and I loved to be invited along. Never discouraged by my limited success, I enjoyed the sense of flying across the water at exhilarating speed. Most times I lost my balance and fell flat on my face, but it was fun anyway. We all wanted Aimee to experience some of that fun too. But it had to be safe above all else.

168

Since I knew little about the sport, I began to ask what I believed to be appropriate questions. I could tell I was annoying the man who was setting up the skis. He was impatient and uninterested in explaining the details and minimized my concerns. Janise asked me to do this because she trusted my judgment. I needed to be sure I trusted my own judgment as well. I needed more information to be sure it was safe. I would never put Aimee in danger. "Don't worry about it!" the man snapped. "Nothing's going to happen to her and there is *no way* she can fall out of the seat!" His response was too flippant and made me even more anxious.

I began talking to another man who had actually engineered and manufactured the adaptive seats being used. His son had cerebral palsy, too. He explained that the ski seat was constructed from a welded metal frame bent and shaped like the bucket seat of a car. In fact, it looked like the kind of welded seat a driver would use in a race car. It even had padded vinyl across the bottom. The child was placed in the seat in a sitting, tilted-back position. Once in the seat, the child essentially sat in the water below the water line. The child's feet were protected in front by wide skis that were attached to the bottom and each side of the seat. Some of the seats were fitted with a small pontoon on each side to provide buoyancy and stability on the water. When pulled by the boat, the skis would glide on the water, lifting the seat upward and back. The child had to grab hold of the towrope that was fed through a front opening in the frame. If the child was unable or incapable of holding the towrope, as in Aimee's case, it was secured to the frame with clamps and knots. Aimee's arms would remain free.

I scrutinized everything and concluded that it appeared safe, especially since Aimee would wear a life vest. Aimee did not swim but very much enjoyed being in the water. Janise, Chloe, and Jeffrey walked closer to observe. Janise asked me what I thought.

"Well, it appears safe. One of the men assured me that she could not fall out and promised they would go slow," I said. I admitted to her that I was still apprehensive and thought perhaps I was being too overprotective. She agreed. When Aimee's name was called, Janise turned to me. "You take her," she said. "I'll wait right here."

"Are you sure we should do this? Do you think she'll be all right?"
I asked.

But before Janise could answer, they called us again. Mel lifted
Aimee out of her chair and carried her to the water's edge, where he
placed her into a seat selected for her size and ability. I held her hand
and stayed with her as they prepared her seat. I noticed it had small
pontoons on the side and thought that was good. The man in charge
handed her the towrope, surprising me because Aimee's arms were
pulled tight against her chest and her hands were in her ever-present
closed-fist position. It seemed to me that he would have immediately
noticed and concluded that Aimee couldn't possibly hold on to the
rope. Even so, I explained that she couldn't see and was incapable of
holding on to the rope and wouldn't know what to do. He glared at me,
then clamped and securely knotted the rope to the seat's frame.

Aimee shivered in the cool water as she threw her arms up, confused, not knowing what was expected of her. She was a little tense, but
with assurance and encouragement relaxed in the seat. She appeared
to comprehend what I said she was going to do and assured me she
wanted to do it. She was ready to go.

I repeated my request that the boat driver take off very slow initially
to give her a little ride around the cove until she could adapt and gain
some confidence. "Oh yeah, they'll go slow," the man said. "She'll be
fine. Just don't worry yourself; she's going to love it!"

I wasn't convinced and I trembled with worry and apprehension. I
explained again that she didn't swim and that she had never done this
before; that I didn't want her to get scared or it would ruin the entire
day, not to mention any future water sports. Chloe was curious and had
come out in the water to see what was going on and grabbed hold of
Mel's hand to watch. Janise watched from the beach. We were all curious how Aimee would react.

"Okay, she's ready to go! Step away!" the man yelled.

"Wait! Wait!" I cried. "She's not strapped in!"

"Oh, we don't strap them in; they could drown if it flips over." He
said. "If she's strapped in, she can't get out. She's wearing a life jacket.
She's safe!"

170

At that moment I was panic-stricken and didn't believe a word he said.

"No, no, no. She cannot do it!" I said. "She arches herself really far back. She is very strong and might push herself out of the seat!"

"Impossible!" he replied. "That's never happened to anyone before. The force of the boat will hold her in her seat. There's no way she can push herself out." He began to push the seat and Aimee away from the shore. Shaking, I was holding on, not daring to let go.

"Are you positive the boat will go slow?" Irritated, he assured me that they all heard my request. I looked at Janise and Mel. They couldn't hear a word being said but by their gestures clearly wondered what was going on. Why the delay? I turned to Mel and shouted that she was not strapped in. He understood and shook his head. "It's okay," he yelled.

Still holding on, I *almost* pulled Aimee out of the seat to abort the ride, but didn't. The boat was revving up and slowly inching forward to tighten the rope. In an instant, it was too late. I fell back as the man next to me gave a "thumbs up" signal to the boat. He hit the throttle with full force and the boat flew forward, zooming toward the middle of the lake!

Aimee, still in the seat, screamed in terror, as her arms waved wildly in the air! The seat began swinging side to side, flying rapidly out of control as it skimmed the water.

"Oh, my God!" I screamed in panic. The boat was going way too fast and did not circle the cove as I requested; instead, it was heading straight for the center of the lake. Janise and Mel ran into the water to be by my side. Stunned, I grabbed Janise as we helplessly watched what happened next.

Aimee continued to scream at the top of her lungs. Her back arched and she was flailing and thrashing about. To our horror, she pushed herself right out of the seat and swung herself violently and uncontrollably over the edge into the water. She didn't float; instead, terrorized, she remained attached to the seat as the boat continued to move, dragging her behind it. Then suddenly the boat stopped and circled around.

Too distant to see exactly what happened, we were certain she was drowning. We felt helpless! We *were* helpless! We could see someone on the boat jump into the water to lift her out. With our hands over our faces and shaking with fear, we thanked God when we heard her cry out. I wondered what I had done. Why did I let her go? When it didn't feel right, I just knew something would happen. It was too late now, and I was infuriated with myself. She could have drowned. I should have listened to my intuition!

When the boat approached the shore, we were relieved to see Aimee sitting on a man's lap. She wasn't crying. In fact, she was talking and laughing with the parents on the boat. What a relief. She was safe! "That's the last time she does that!" Janise exclaimed. "Yes," I agreed. Mel ran out to meet the boat. He carried Aimee out of the water and carefully placed her in her wheelchair. Immensely relieved, we all hugged and kissed her and returned to our camp, but not before I excused myself to have a few words with the men in charge. Their lack of concern for Aimee's limitations could have caused her serious bodily harm or even killed her.

Fear for Aimee's life had worn me out. My energy had been zapped and I was ready to go home. The kids were hungry, and we decided to try to calm down and have lunch. We watched the other children ski while we ate. Aimee still had three or four more turns to ski, but when they called us a second time we passed. We definitely weren't going to do that again. It was simply far too dangerous for Aimee, no matter how safe for other children.

"How about just a ride in the boat?" one of the men asked me. I told him we would think about it while Mel took Aimee to play in the water with Chloe and Jeffrey. Janise and I discussed the man's offer as we packed our things. We agreed that it would be constructive for Aimee to end the day on a positive note. Past experience had taught us that this kind of occurrence could leave Aimee fearful of water even to the point of not wanting to take a bath.

Her turn to ski came up again, and Mel carried her into the waist-high water, where she was picked up by another man and carried to the waiting boat. She was poised and self-assured and wanted to ride

172

in the boat again. Suddenly, Janise ran into the water. "I'm going with her," she said. When the boat returned Aimee was smiling and happy.

"I rode in the boat!" she shouted.

I was impressed with Aimee's ability to overcome a potentially dev-astating experience. Taking Aimee to a new and unfamiliar activity always involves risk. On a routine day we must constantly be on guard that she doesn't fall, that she is securely positioned and strapped in her chair, and that the wheelchair brakes are locked when they need to be. We also have to continually pay attention to what and how she eats and drinks to ensure she doesn't choke. Aimee can verbalize her wants and needs, but her caretaker must assume full responsibility for her at all times, since she is physically fragile and basically helpless.

As we drove away from the lake, Janise mentioned that the same group also organized winter activities. "They do snow skiing for these kids also," she said. "Maybe that would be better for Aimee."

"Janise, I don't know about that," I laughed. "It's going to take me awhile to feel comfortable enough to take her to do anything like this again." Knowing Aimee, she would be ready and willing to try anything new. At that moment though, all I could visualize was Aimee in some sort of adaptive contraption flying down a hillside of snow, screaming, and out of control. No, I wasn't ready to do that . . . yet.

• • •

On August 21, 2005, Aimee's eighth birthday, we headed to Southern California for another therapy session. Staffing problems had short-ened this session to three and a half weeks instead of the usual four. That schedule was fine with me, because we wanted to complete the session before school started. Scheduling therapy sessions during the school year is not desirable, but sometimes it's unavoidable. Arrange-ments are made months in advance and require careful preparation, planning, and commitment. Venue availability, logistics, personal and social obligations, business responsibilities, and Aimee's school schedule are all important considerations.

We welcomed Mel's company on our drive south but had to give up the loud music. Aimee enjoys music most when it is turned up full blast. Mel doesn't. It didn't occur to me at first why Aimee kept asking who was going to drive. Then I got it. "Aimee, why are you so concerned about who drives the car?" I asked. She threw her head back and laughed. "Grammy, I like it when you drive because the music is loud!" She had correctly concluded that whoever was at the wheel also had control of the music system. She knew she could depend on me to play her favorite CDs—and play them loud.

Listening to music is probably Aimee's favorite activity, anywhere, anytime. To keep my sanity, I developed a system for listening to music on long drives. We start with something fast and upbeat, such as rock and Latin music. Next is easy listening, like jazz or instrumental. That is followed by what I call "quiet music" such as opera or classical. After that, Aimee is receptive to an auditory time-out while she dozes or sleeps. For the last portion of the trip, as Aimee becomes a little impatient, I crank up the music again in anticipation of reaching our destination. There is a psychology to this and it actually works. Aimee, of course, picks the artists in each category. She knows exactly who she wants to listen to and insists that her selections are played. She merrily sings along and keeps beat with the music.

As soon as we are in the car, settled in and ready to go, Aimee is quick to remind us that the music is not on. From the backseat she whispers, "Grammy, I want something." She will repeat this several times until she is acknowledged. "Speak up, Aimee, I can't hear you," I say. She whispers again and laughs. We both know what she wants. "Muuuuuuuusic!" she finally says. And so the conversation goes, until the music is turned on and her selections are made. If she likes the CD already in the player, she will smile and keep beat or sing. If it is not what she wants, she will let you know and continue to let you know until she has her way.

Traveling south on Highway 5 is boring and we always plan a stop at Harris Ranch for lunch. Located in the middle of nowhere, although close to Bakersfield, it is a nice place to enjoy a meal before proceeding over the "Grapevine" into the Los Angeles basin. That day, in the restaurant, an elderly Asian woman approached our table. She wanted to know about Aimee. She said that Aimee had an "aura" about her and she wanted to meet her. Of course, Aimee talks to everyone and this woman was no exception. The woman told us she was a "spiritual healer" from Los Angeles and suggested we take Aimee to her during our stay in Southern California. She presented Mel with her card and insisted she could help Aimee. Mel listened; I did not. "No way!" I told Mel. "We're not doing that." Spiritual healing may have credence, but this was someone I knew nothing about. I had no intention of taking Aimee to see her. In fact, I thought it offensive that she approached us at all. My impression was that she probably hit on handicapped kids and their seemingly desperate parents.

• • •

Aimee's therapy began the following day. She was eager to get started and see everyone again. We arrived at the center early so Aimee would have time to greet everyone with the usual hugs and kisses. She loves reunions and everyone was delighted when she remembered them by name. But this time Bret wasn't there. Aimee was assigned to a new male therapist named Rolf and immediately connected with him. "Hi, Rolf, I like you." Then, turning to me, she said, "Grammy, look at Rolf. Look at him. He's so cute! Do you think he's cute, Grammy?"

There are often occasions when Aimee can make embarrassing comments—innocent, but inappropriate. This was one of those times. Rolf turned beet red as he responded, "I like you, too, Aimee and we're going to have fun working together." In truth, Rolf was a handsome young man from Poland. He came to the United States as a youth, returned to Poland to earn his degree in physical therapy, and then returned to California, where he now lived with his wife. It was good that Aimee liked him. This motivated her work.

During this session, the treatment plan included working with Aimee's new walker. It was delivered and fitted while we were there. Rolf worked with her in her walker for one hour each day. The therapy session was a huge success. Every day following the suit therapy, Rolf and I would strap Aimee in her body brace and lock her in position on the walker. Seeking attention, she wanted everyone to watch what she was doing. "Look at me, look at me, I'm walking!" she said over and over. She couldn't wait to get out the door and walk around the complex.

Rolf solicited my help for this portion of the therapy, and I eagerly complied as he directed Aimee. He required her to count aloud and pace herself rhythmically for each and every step. He explained that the brain shuts down when overloaded. And that was what happened to Aimee when she would take a few steps then stop, her head and arms drooping and limp. Suddenly, with head erect, smiling, she would resume walking.

Most of us take steps without thinking, but for Aimee it was different. The walker tension was adjusted so that each step required tremendous concentration and strength. The goal, Rolf explained, was to keep Aimee walking without stopping so that the brain "patterned" stepping in rhythm.

"Look, Rolf, look at me," she'd say. Rolf ignored her. He insisted that she and we not talk during these sessions. Instead he and I communicated with hand and eye signals only. If Aimee heard us talking about anything, she would enter the conversation, thus breaking her concentration. For that reason, not a word was spoken. Aimee would often stop, turn her head, and listen intently. Nothing. Then she would laugh out loud.

Nothing. It was difficult not to respond or laugh at her funny remarks, but this was serious business and there was no place for humor or games. We often turned our backs so she couldn't see us laughing at what she said. Rolf would have me walk to a far end of the walkway and wait. He encouraged Aimee to look forward and to walk in the direction where she was looking. This was important. Aimee cannot see very well. Knowing that, he wanted her to draw a visual line to where she was going.

At the end of three weeks, Aimee was able to walk around the complex without stopping, counting "one, two; one, two; one, two," as she walked. She couldn't walk enough! Her body, however, could only tolerate one hour in the walker. She was worn out and weak when it came off.

Often barely able to stay awake during lunch, she asked if she could take a nap—an indication of how fatigued she really was. Aimee was unwavering in her desire to please Rolf. She never cried or complained but instead worked harder and harder each day. Her resolve won Rolf's admiration and respect.

Rolf proved to be an excellent therapist. Unfortunately, the administrative policies at the center were stressful and frustrating. Schedules were changed daily without notice, and parents argued with each other because of it. I remained focused on Aimee and her therapy and refused to get involved in the politics of the center. Sometimes it was difficult to ignore and wore my patience thin.

I made Aimee's requirements absolutely clear prior to our arrival. I expected a guarantee from the owner regarding two matters of importance to me: First, Aimee was to be scheduled for the morning, and second, she was to have the same therapist for the entire time. Change disrupted Aimee's concentration and progress. I made it clear that without these guarantees, Aimee would not attend, and the owner agreed. Some parents lived in the vicinity of the center and had greater flexibility in scheduling. I did not have that flexibility and had to make our time productive; once there I could not simply switch our program to another week or month.

One day, Gay, the owner of the center, invited me to see the wares of a Chinese importer who had set up a temporary showroom at a local mall. During a previous session, she had taken me to a wholesaler in Pasadena who had some interesting old and new Chinese objets d' art. At that time, I had purchased several items for my store, but now I had no desire to purchase anything because I had closed my store. I explained and she understood. But, as a shrewd entrepreneur, I was certain arrangements were made with these vendors for compensation. She wanted me to buy. As a courtesy, I agreed to go when she insisted. She drove Aimee and me there one afternoon immediately following therapy.

The drive took over an hour, and when we finally arrived at the mall Aimee was drained and hungry. The only restaurant available was a Chinese restaurant, which was fine with Aimee. Gay made the menu selections and was flabbergasted at Aimee's appetite and the gusto with which she ate. Aimee delighted in Gay's conversation with the server and, listening, said, "Grammy, Gay is talking Chinese! I can talk Chinese, too." I knew what Aimee would do next. When she made sounds that to her sounded like "Chinese," we all laughed.

After lunch, we checked out the merchandise displayed by Gay's friend. Underimpressed with the selections, I still felt obliged to buy something and selected a small bowl for my daughter. Gay continued to walk me around and around the display several times encouraging me to buy. Finally, accepting that there was nothing of interest to me, and nothing more to buy, we left.

When Gay returned us to the therapy center and our SUV back in Anaheim, we thanked her for the afternoon and said good-bye. Within minutes of her departure, Aimee turned to me and said, "Grammy, Gay doesn't like you!" I laughed at her remark and said nothing. I started the car and drove to our hotel. Again, on the way, Aimee commented, "Grammy, I *told* you Gay doesn't like you!"

"Why are you saying that, Aimee?" I inquired, a little irritated. "Of course she likes me, I'm her friend."

"No, no, no. *She doesn't like you!* She told me, she told me in her head!"

I was convinced Aimee's assessment and intuition had told her something. I never had the impression that Gay didn't like me, but perhaps Aimee had it right . . . perhaps Gay didn't like me after all.

• • •

One day during a morning break, Aimee told me that one of the mothers, Lucy, "talked too much" and that "other people don't like it." Always alert and listening intently to every conversation within earshot, Aimee was accurate in her perception and remarks. Lucy did like to talk and had a great sense of humor, at least, in my opinion. I enjoyed her, but perhaps she wasn't as entertaining to everyone as I thought. Even so, I was impressed with Aimee's perceptiveness.

Our session was drawing to a close and I began to prepare for our departure. This had been another productive session for Aimee. Her confidence was at an all-time high, and she was proud of her accomplishments. I was proud of her achievements and impressed with her focus and unrelenting desire to do well. Most of all, I marveled at her maturity and cognition. Her ability to communicate with others was remarkable. She had gained in every way.

$$\bullet \;\; \bullet \;\; \bullet$$

In two days, everything in our room was packed and boxed. We left the following morning at 5:30 a.m. Our early departure paid off as we zipped through Los Angeles, avoiding the morning commute. We headed north on the scenic and picturesque Highway 1. Stopping for breaks and lunch along the way, Aimee enjoyed the change of pace and was eager to see her family again. She asked me several times, "Who will be waiting for me in Modesto, Grammy?"

"Everyone who loves you," I assured her.

THE GIFTS

THAT OCTOBER, Mel and I took a long-awaited vacation to Sicily. I was eager to evaluate my ability to travel abroad following my heart attack. This trip would provide me with a test of my stamina. Travel to Poland with Aimee required absolute confidence on my part, and the trip to Sicily eliminated any doubt in my mind that I could do it.

We returned home in November rested and reenergized. The holiday season was already in full swing and I began to think about Christmas for the family. I wanted to do something special for the grandchildren that year—not money, not a toy, but something really meaningful and memorable. I thought about the gift of a life experience instead. Chloe had been talking about New York City for months. It was her dream to go there, and she mentioned it often in her conversations with me. One day she said, "Aimee always gets to go away on trips with you, Grammy, and I never get to do that!"

"Chloe," I said, "you are right. But when Grammy and Aimee travel it is work, not the same as a vacation." Still, what she said was true. "Maybe I can plan something for just the two of us. I'll think about it." She was happy with my comments and told me it would please her very much if we could do that.

Traveling to new places, especially in an airplane, and spending time together is always a great experience. Chloe was too young to understand entirely, but she grasped enough to know that she wasn't included when Aimee and I traveled. I explained many times to Chloe that when I took Aimee, it gave her parents a chance to do things with her that they would otherwise not be able to do. But no matter how caring, interested, and involved I had been in all of Chloe's activities, it still wasn't enough. It was not quality one-on-one time, and that's what she was asking for. Her comment tore at my heart.

It was time for me to make time for the other grandkids, but how? They were each involved in their own world and activities—but the truth was I had not been as involved with them as much as I should have, certainly not as much as I had been with Aimee. After much thought, I decided to organize a special trip for each grandchild. I became completely engrossed in this new endeavor and prepared a specific travel gift to match each child's special interests.

Chloe knew a lot about New York City. In fact, she knew a lot about many things that I'd had no clue about when I was eight. Where she obtained so much information about the city remained a mystery to me, but she made it clear that she wanted to go there some day. Exuberant and bright as the lights on Broadway, Chloe was ready for the Big Apple. Dramatic and confident, I thought she was old enough to appreciate and enjoy a trip together.

• • •

Jeffrey, now almost five, also had never spent a weekend alone with us. Quiet, reserved, and reluctant to leave home in the past, he seemed old enough now to have some fun away from home. We knew Jeffrey enjoyed the outdoors and nature, in particular. He is a curious and extremely creative child, often writing notes, drawing pictures, and sculpting animals and characters in the stories he makes up. Like most boys his age, he was fascinated with dinosaurs. This was a starting point in planning his gift.

I discussed my ideas with Mel, who agreed that it would be wonderful to give each child a trip. We decided that I would take Chloe, alone, to New York City for a week; Mel and I would take Aimee to Hawaii with us for a week; and we would both take Jeffrey for a "nature" weekend, complete with hiking and visiting a natural history museum to see dinosaurs.

My heart attack had changed me. I felt strongly that if anything happened to me, I wanted each grandchild to have had an experience with me that they could savor. This was especially true for Chloe and Jeffrey, since they had not had the opportunity, in my opinion, to spend the quality time with us that they deserved and needed.

• • •

Previously, we had alternated Christmas Eve and Christmas Day activities each year so that our children were together on one day or the other. When Jason and Janise moved to Modesto, we changed our annual Christmas routine and got together for the entire day on the Sunday before Christmas. This arrangement was not my first choice, but it still works out very well and actually gives us a day to enjoy the children and to focus on the joy of simply being together for Christmas without being rushed or burned out.

The Christmas holiday that year would be special. First, I planned a treasure hunt for the kids. The clues about their gifts included a CD with a song that would hint at where they were going. I spent hours finding just the right music to download for each CD. With other related gifts, I also planned to include a poem that I had written specifically for each child with keywords that offered them clues about their trips. I awoke at all hours of the night with rhymes and ideas in my head for the poems. With paper and pencil next to my bed, I wrote down my thoughts as they came to me. I was as excited as a kid.

• • •

Finally, the day arrived. The children couldn't wait to get started and anticipated something special but didn't know what. Jeffrey ran wildly about, and Chloe pushed Aimee through the house as they raced to find their clues, the box containing the treasure, and the three envelopes inside.

Each envelope had a name and a CD. Chloe's CD had Frank Sinatra's "New York, New York." Aimee's CD had her favorite Elvis Presley, singing "Blue Hawaii." Jeffrey's CD had a group singing, "The Dinosaur Stomp."

Chloe was first. She cautiously opened her envelope. Shaking, she listened to the CD. She was delighted but didn't say a word as her mouth opened in a silent scream and her hands covered her face. Then she smiled, and in typical Chloe fashion, struck a pose for a photo!

We watched and waited and she opened the poem. Still shaking, she couldn't read it, so her dad read it to her:

THE BIG APPLE

It's called the "Big Apple" but not one you eat.
Statues, buildings, and cabs,
Oh what a treat!

Shopping and Broadway
We'll go to a show,
And then I will test you
For how much you know!

NBC and the *Today* show that you will see,
Our family might watch us on the TV.
Metropolitan Museum and a ride in the park,
We'll need to be careful when it gets dark!

The month of January it's snowy and cold,
To be at that time one must be bold.
It's called New York City

**And that's where you'll be
We're going to go there
Just you and me!**

Chloe was delirious with joy, ecstatic that she would finally see the city of her heart's desire. She opened her wrapped gift box and was thrilled to find first-class round-trip tickets to New York City; a children's travel guide; tickets and brochures to the Statue of Liberty, Empire State Building, and a Broadway play—*Beauty and the Beast*. For Chloe it was a dream come true. The delight on her face reflected the happiness I knew she felt in her heart. And holding her tickets in hand, she posed for another photo. I smiled and rejoiced in the moment.

• • •

Jeffrey's turn was next. He was excited and eager to get to his gifts. A very bright, sensitive, and creative four-year-old, he loved to explore and learn new things. Mel and I had not really spent much time alone with Jeffrey up to this point, and I hoped our weekend adventure would give us an opportunity to learn more about each other.

There is a four-year age gap between Jeffrey and the twins. During his infancy I spent most of my available time primarily focused on Aimee and Chloe. Part of that was simply because of living out of town; even so, I never really had enjoyed quality time with him as an infant or toddler. This was a big disappointment to me because there simply never seemed to be enough time. Now he was suddenly in school and I felt a sense of remorse and regret that I hadn't done more. I hoped it wasn't too late to nourish a better relationship with him.

He listened with enthusiasm to his CD and began to "stomp" with the music, not really understanding what it meant. Next, Mel handed him a big remote-controlled dinosaur standing on a stack of books all wrapped in plastic and a big bow. He opened his envelope and handed me the paper inside.

"Grammy, will you read it for me, please?" he asked. I read his poem:

THE DINOSAUR STOMP

Go to the "dino" and find him all wrapped.
He looks like a mummy and fits in your lap!
He's only a "dino" but he's pretty hip.
You'll be happy to learn you're taking a trip!

A day or a weekend, you'll tell us so
And we'll learn how they found them so long ago.
At the museum, a hike in the park.
We can stay all day until it gets dark.

You'll learn about "dinos"
And all that they were.
The dinosaur museum—
We're taking you there!

Jeffrey is extremely bright, curious, and always eager to learn new things. He has several books about dinosaurs, insects, and other natural exploration activities. He was overjoyed in anticipation of his weekend. We planned to hike and search for fossils, but most of all, he couldn't wait to see real dinosaur bones. He threw his arms around us in appreciation and affection.

Aimee was last. She knew everyone was excited about something but didn't quite get the entire picture. She listened to her CD and began to sing with Elvis. She had heard the song before she knew the words but didn't understand the significance now. Then I read her poem and explained it in detail:

GOING TO HAWAII

The flowers are fragrant
In the air you will smell,
Oh, it's a surprise
I'm not going to tell!

You will like the music,
And shake your "cula."
The way that they dance
Is called the "hula."

Get to your box and open it quick,
Look inside and you will see . . .
When it comes to March
Where you will be!

Sea and land filled with bright sun,
We're going to Hawaii
And know you'll have fun!

She kept saying, "Guess what? I'm going to Hawaii with Grammy and Tutu!" Sharing her joy, we responded with smiles and laughter. Janise helped her open her gift box, which contained round-trip tickets to Hawaii, a lei, a children's guide to Hawaii, and brochures from the Royal Hawaiian Hotel, where we would stay.

Christmas this year had a special significance for me. Each day of my life had to count, and I had reached a point where I could share something meaningful with each of my precious and adored grandchildren. Sharing part of me, with an original poem and an adventure, was a start—one I hoped would continue for many years to follow.

Chloe began the countdown almost immediately. We departed for New York right after the holiday on January 4. I deliberately planned our arrival in time to see the beautifully decorated store windows, the magnificent Rockefeller Center Christmas tree, and the bright lights setting the city aglow in holiday splendor.

Chloe and I shared a suite at the Benjamin Hotel in Manhattan. Feeling sophisticated and mature, Chloe adored having her own room. Dressed comfortably in our jeans and boots and keeping warm in long coats, hats, and gloves, we walked from one end of Manhattan to the other. We rode the subway and took a cab to Broadway at night. The magic of the American Girl doll store, the thrill of the Ferris wheel inside the Toys R Us store, and the tapping piano keys on the floor at FAO Schwartz kept a smile on Chloe's face.

We did New York right: Chloe ice-skated at Rockefeller Center. We stood in line at 5:00 a.m. for the *Today* show in hopes of being on television. Chloe waited patiently for the camera to scan her as she smiled and waved and held up the sign she'd made and brought from home. We peered out at the city from the top of the Empire State Building. Most memorable was the day we spent visiting the Statue of Liberty, followed by a walk to Ground Zero. We arrived at the location where the towers had been and peered through the fence at the deep hole left where they once stood. We looked at the photos attached to the wall— each notice and poster was heartbreaking. We held hands and cried as we read them together. Touched and deeply moved, Chloe had many questions about how and why it happened, which we discussed over lunch followed by a long walk to Times Square.

Uninterrupted time together gave us an opportunity to bond. With no restrictions to hold us back, we relished each day. We enjoyed our talks as we walked to the local corner café for our morning coffee and hot chocolate and chatted over hotdogs and French fries from Chloe's favorite street vendor.

We attended mass at St. Patrick's Cathedral on Sunday morning and looked in awe at the wonder and detail of the magnificent nativity scene. A carriage ride to Tavern on the Green for lunch and a walk to the Metropolitan Museum concluded our holiday in New York City. We had a wonderful time.

• • •

Jeffrey's weekend followed a few weeks later. Janna and Greg lived in the area and joined us for our outing. We took Jeffrey to Sacramento to the Sierra College Natural History Museum. He listened intently to every word as Mel explained the museum's exhibit. Next we had a long hike through the forest, where Jeffrey left no stone unturned as he examined every nook and cranny along the trail.

The experience of staying in a hotel and eating out in restaurants with us was a treat, as acknowledged by Jeffrey's good manners, independence, and maturity for his age. It was a significant weekend in developing a long overdue meaningful relationship and bonding time with this darling, very bright, little boy.

. . .

Soon March arrived and it was time to take Aimee to Hawaii. Mel was eager to visit his family, who still lived on the island of Oahu, where he had grown up. They had all met Aimee when she was an infant years before and were amazed when they saw her now. She adored talking with Mel's brothers, Mike and Dean, and flirted with them when they came to our hotel.

The fragrance in the air when we arrived at the airport in Honolulu immediately caught Aimee's attention. She took deep breaths and smelled the flowers. Mel looked forward to bringing Aimee to Hawaii and especially enjoyed time with her. This was his home, and he wanted to share it with her and make sure she enjoyed all the activities available to her.

He took her into the warm ocean waters and lay with her on the beach. He never did this at home, but for Aimee he would remain outdoors for hours, reading and talking as they enjoyed the warm Hawaiian sun. Mel took her swimming in the hotel pool, where she splashed and played with the other children, after which they dozed together in lounge chairs under pink umbrellas. I sat with them by the pool and observed Aimee's interaction with the other children.

What I saw made me happy—but sad, too. Aimee was so outgoing and friendly and wanted desperately to connect with children around her. But unless the children were infants or toddlers, they stared at her, whispered, and wondered why someone had to hold her in the water and why she moved and behaved the way she did. They knew she was different, but Aimee didn't always seem to know that about herself. She ignored their often perplexed and sometimes frightened reactions at her attempts to converse with them. Aimee was having a great time.

Her limited sight, I hoped, protected her from their stares and contemptuous expressions.

Aimee loved the food in Hawaii. She smacked her lips at the sweet juicy taste of the tropical fruits and especially enjoyed the delicious fruit drinks at the patio bar. Chinese food is one of Aimee's favorites and the tasty and spicy dim sum morsels topped her list. Mel's brothers always take us to new cutting-edge restaurants in Honolulu. Aimee impressed everyone with her good manners, her understanding of food ingredients offered on the menu, and her appetite. One afternoon we drove across the island to eat the specials at a popular outdoor shack where they cooked hot and spicy shrimp served on paper plates. Mel ordered the mild version, but Aimee and I burned our lips and I licked my fingers as we enjoyed the tangy, hot shrimp.

One day while driving to the Museum of Art in Honolulu, we passed the large Mormon Temple. The lushly landscaped gardens impressed me and I casually commented to Mel about the beautiful, yet unusual, architecture of the structure. Aimee, in the backseat, offered her unsolicited comments. "Jacka goes to the Mormons!" Jacka is what Aimee often calls her other grandmother, Janise's mother, Jackie.

"Jacka goes to the Mormons too, Grammy!" she said again. I looked at Mel and shrugged my shoulders. "I thought Jackie was Catholic," I said to Mel. "I didn't know she goes to the Mormon church, did you?" Mel looked at me, perplexed as well, and said he didn't think so. We giggled at Aimee's comment as she continued to make her point.

"Grammy, Grammy, I *said* Jacka goes to the Mormons! She goes to the Mormons in Modesto!" Finally, I turned completely around to face her and asked, "Aimee, how do you know that Jackie goes to the Mormon church? I think you're mistaken."

She bristled at my comment. "No! No! Grammy, she *goes* to the Mormons! She *goes* to the Mormons at the *mall*!"

"What Mormons at the mall? There are no Mormons at the mall, Aimee." I said, annoyed.

"Oh yes, she does, Grammy! Jacka goes *shopping* at the Mormons at the mall!"

She insisted. What was she talking about? I couldn't figure it out. Then I thought about the keywords here, "mall" and "shopping." It suddenly occurred to me and I asked, "Aimee, do you mean *Mervyns* at the mall?" I asked.

"Yes, that's right! Jacka shops at Mervyns at the mall!

Mel and I laughed. She was so insistent that she was right and, in a way she was. Why didn't I get it? What I did get, though, was affirmation that Aimee listened to everything said in her presence. She wanted to contribute to the conversation and, as evidenced of her attitude, felt she had something to say—persisting until she was heard and understood.

• • •

The evenings in Honolulu were balmy and beautiful. When it wasn't raining we took long walks along Waikiki Beach. Touristy, yes, but for Aimee a delightful chance to explore scents, sounds, people, and lots of action.

Where there is music you will find Aimee. She enjoyed the entertainment every afternoon at the hotel garden lanai. The hula dancers intrigued her as they moved their hands and arms and swayed to the ukulele music. Their colorful dresses caught her attention. It didn't take long for Aimee to become familiar with the words to the typical Hawaiian songs as she happily sang along.

"Grammy, move me closer, please—move me closer *right now!*" she demanded.

I gladly did as she asked, because I knew she couldn't move there by herself. She couldn't dance the hula, but she could swing her arms high while sitting in her chair, in her floral sundress, wearing a bright orchid in her hair "just like the hula dancers."

Our last evening in Hawaii was spent with Mel's cousin, Carol, and her seven-year-old granddaughter, Raymie, who is hearing impaired. Raymie had been told all about Aimee and couldn't wait for us to bring her to Hawaii. Now they would finally meet. We had told Aimee all about her cousin Raymie and she was eager to meet her, as well.

Carol planned an evening of fun for the girls at the local Chuck-E-Cheese pizza parlor—noisy, chaotic, and terrifying for Aimee. But Raymie was excited, and we couldn't disappoint her by telling her we couldn't go. We had to at least give it a try. They didn't know that Aimee absolutely panicked when she walked into any Chuck-E-Cheese or similar venue. Perhaps it was the traumatic birthday party Janise had arranged three years ago for Chloe and Aimee that made it intolerable for her. They had avoided ever taking her there again and took the other children only when Aimee wasn't around.

But I was confident I could work this out with Aimee. I prepared her for the evening by stressing how much fun she was going to have and that Raymie couldn't wait to play games with her and win prizes. Most of all, she could eat her favorite pepperoni pizza for dinner. I avoided telling her the name of the place.

When we arrived, she knew exactly where we were. Distressed, initially, she quickly became enamored of Raymie, who loaded her down with gifts and attention. Raymie was enthusiastic about sharing the evening with Aimee and said, "Come on, Aimee, let's go play games!" I held my breath for a moment in anticipation of a scream, but no scream came. I breathed a sigh of relief as Aimee exclaimed, "Grammy, please take me, I want to go play games with Raymie!" Off we went while Mel got a cup of tokens.

Raymie was dropping tokens into her favorite machine fast and furious. Tickets were spewing out and dropping in a long rope to the floor. Aimee watched and squealed with Raymie each time she made a point. I leisurely walked her around and looked at the games as I tried to solicit her interest in something she could do.

"No, no. I don't like it," she'd say, and off we would go to the next game machine. We circled back around and approached the game Raymie had played earlier. Aimee seemed familiar with it because it was something she had watched Raymie do. It wasn't too noisy or too flashy like some others: The coins dropped off a platform, ringing bells if they landed in a designated circle. Aimee was determined to drop her own tokens in the slot.

This simple task became a challenge, one that tried my patience. Aimee sees on her left side only; therefore, I had to turn her chair parallel to the machine with her left side near the token slot at the front of the machine. Reaching as far as she could, coin very tight in her fist, she felt for the slot as I stretched and pulled her spindly arm as far as it could go.

"I can do it Grammy; I can do it by *myself*!" she insisted. Even though she could not, I encouraged and praised her for doing so. I understood that in her heart she *wanted* to do it alone and be like Raymie. In her own mind, she had done that—even though I assisted; she had done it because she tried.

When the coin dropped into the machine, a circus-like calliope tune began to play as hundreds of tokens on platforms inside the case were raked to and fro. They fell like raindrops and where they fell created more bells and whistles. The expression on Aimee's face was one of triumph at the recognition that she had done it herself. A constant stream of winning ticket coupons spewed from the machine. She was elated with herself and happy she was playing with Raymie. They had a terrific time.

When the larger-than-life mascot, Chuck-E, approached Aimee, I signaled for him to move away. I didn't want him to spoil her time now. Those large characters always freak Aimee out, and they inevitably come up to her chair because they think she will like the attention. Instead, she screams. He was approaching on her sightless side and I thought he would frighten her for sure. But she managed to tolerate the big Chuck-E by her side. I was even able to document the moment with my camera. Later, when the band began to play for a birthday party, Aimee even joined in singing "Happy Birthday" with Raymie and the other children. It's all about sharing, I thought.

Overcoming the fear of loud noises, unfamiliar sounds, and bright lights is insignificant for most children. It was a momentous achievement for Aimee. The panic and trepidation in her eyes earlier in the evening had been replaced with an expression of joy. I shook my head and smiled as I stepped away when she said in her bossy tone, "Grammy, please go sit down *now*. I want *Raymie* to push my chair!" That said it all.

THE RECITAL

THIRD GRADE PRESENTED new challenges for Aimee and she learned to recognize letters and develop her vocabulary. I assembled black and white books under her teacher's direction with simple words such as *cat, hat, dog, dad,* and *mom* written for her in large white letters. In April Aimee was honored at the school assembly with the "Principal's Award for Outstanding Citizenship," which was presented for her learning accomplishments, excellent attitude, and outstanding citizenship toward her teachers and fellow students. Aimee certainly deserved this prestigious recognition, and she inspired fellow students with her example of enthusiasm and dedication to learning.

• • •

Chloe took piano lessons and performed at biannual recitals. Aimee expressed her desire to do the same. She couldn't play an instrument, so I suggested we give Aimee voice lessons so she could participate too. She loved to sing, and whether or not she learned to read music didn't matter; she couldn't see it anyway. Janise inquired at the music school, and they agreed to accept Aimee. We assured them there was no expectation other than for Aimee to have fun in the process. Her teacher, a man, often became frustrated with Aimee's antics, but patiently worked with her. He wanted to prepare her to perform in the spring recital and gave her several songs to rehearse at home. To ensure that she had an opportunity to perform like the other students, he decided to record her singing during a lesson and would play that at the recital if all else failed.

The big night finally arrived. I had bought the girls lovely polka-dot, organza party dresses with big pink sashes. Chloe reminded me that this would be the perfect occasion to wear them. They did not dress alike for school, but sometimes, for special occasions, they wore the same outfits. They were adorable in the dresses with pink bows in their pulled-up hair, big brown eyes, long eyelashes, and big smiles.

Aimee had attended these recitals before, but because she had so many comments to make during the performance, Mel often sat in the rear, ready to remove her from the auditorium so that she didn't disrupt others. Her critiques of each performance, often said loudly, were frank and could be anything from "her voice stinks" to "what beautiful music."

On this particular evening, she was ready for the recital and sat in the aisle next to me, looking lovely. Janise sat in front of us because she thought Aimee would focus better sitting next to me. I coached her and encouraged her to sing when the music began. She was introduced when her instructor said, "Ladies and gentlemen, tonight we have an unusual, but special performance . . ." as he pointed her out in the aisle. He had already decided earlier not to even try to have her sing on stage.

All eyes were upon her as the prelude to her music began. Her lips quivered for a moment, and then she heard her own voice on the loudspeaker singing "Twinkle, Twinkle, Little Star." She began to sing with her own recording. There wasn't a dry eye in the audience as she received a standing ovation for her performance. She turned to me and said, "Grammy, my heart is full of joy! I'm so happy to be here!"

• • •

Aimee was preparing to make her First Holy Communion with Chloe. This major achievement was carried out in May 2006, in a morning mass at their family parish in Modesto. Chloe had religion classes at school, and it was routine that her class would make their Communion together. Aimee, on the other hand, went to public school and had no religious exposure in her day-to-day curriculum.

One day I asked Janise if Aimee would be able to receive this sacrament in the ceremony with Chloe's class. She was told that it was doubtful Aimee would be able to do so. "Janise," I said, "you'll have to figure out a way; they came into the world together, were baptized together, and they should make their First Communion together too."

She agreed. As the time approached, I encouraged her to follow up with the new priest at their parish. Luckily, he approved. Aimee would be required to attend several catechism retreats in preparation for the sacrament. Chloe attended the classes with her and later told us how embarrassed she had been because Aimee was so demonstrative. When the instructor asked the group questions to test their religious knowledge, the children remained silent. Aimee, quickly responding to various questions she knew nothing about, would raise her hand saying, "I know! I know!" Aimee then would say, "I forgot!" Everyone would laugh, including Chloe, but especially Aimee.

Gaining control of the situation, and enjoying the attention, Aimee repeatedly interrupted by saying, "Miss Teacher, I have a question." Chloe, in good humor and entertained by Aimee's remarks, laughed heartily when she told me, "Oh Grammy, Aimee is so embarrassing, but she's so hilarious. I just love when she makes everyone laugh!" I'm sure this makes her sad at times, too.

At the final retreat, the children were given a "host" and sacramental wine in preparation of the ceremony. Aimee buttoned up her lips in protest as she refused the host but exclaimed, "I'll drink the wine!"

The girls wore matching white dresses for the occasion. Aimee, fond of dresses and with a penchant for hair ribbons, would be satisfied with anything pretty. Chloe, athletic and particular about what she wore, was more difficult to please—so she made the selection of their outfits.

We arrived in Modesto on Saturday to prepare for the event on Sunday morning. Janise and I took the girls shopping for white ballerina-type shoes. After dinner, Aimee returned to the hotel with us. Janise had house guests, so I gladly dressed Aimee for the occasion. Janise was surprised in the morning when I told her Aimee had slept through the night with sponge rollers in her hair. This was a first, but Aimee cooperated because she enjoys primping and looking "pretty for her daddy."

Friends and family converged on the church and took over the front row, where arrangements were made to accommodate Aimee's wheelchair. The procession began. Janise rolled Aimee up the aisle first, Chloe at her side, leading the way for the other children, marching in pairs—the girls in white dresses and veils, the boys in suits and ties.

There was not a dry eye in the congregation as the children came in. The music stopped and the ceremony began. The priest asked questions of the children. Without giving Aimee time to interrupt, he deliberately asked her one pointed question that required a simple answer, "Do you love Jesus?" She proudly responded, "Yes, I do."

The ceremony was lovely and Aimee was doing well until it was time to receive the consecrated bread and wine. We held our breaths in anticipation of what she might do. Screaming, she buttoned her lips, shook her head, and refused the host. Janise, sitting next to me, implored me to do something. Mortified, I walked up, took the host from the Eucharistic minister, and said, "I'll give it to her in a moment." When she returned to the pew and settled down, I was able to give her a small piece so she could complete this religious rite and receive the grace of the sacrament.

A party followed at a local restaurant where Aimee and Chloe were the guests of honor. Beautiful girls, they remained side by side as they greeted each guest with a kiss. I looked at them, together, darling angels, the same but different, and thought what a truly wonderful blessing this day had been.

• • •

I arranged for a return trip to Poland. Feeling confident I could make the trip with Aimee and feeling strong physically, I scheduled us for the May–June session. Near the conclusion of the school year, Aimee would not have to miss much school and the spring weather would be pleasant. We left on May 8 from San Francisco and were scheduled to arrive at Euromed on May 9 for evaluations. Revised flight schedules provided us with a new option for travel from San Francisco to New York to Berlin. In Berlin, we were met by the dependable and reliable Christian, who drove us to Mielno.

· · ·

Our close friend Monsignor Browne, at the Basilica Cathedral in San Jose, prayed for Aimee and me daily and said mass for us often. On the morning of our departure he graciously gifted us with a special blessing for a successful and safe journey. Aimee had met him before when he joined us for coffee at the Fairmont Hotel lobby, across the street from the Cathedral. She liked him a lot and recalled him immediately. As he was performing the blessing, she kept asking him if he liked coffee. He looked at her oddly and smiled. He didn't get it, but I knew exactly what Aimee was aiming for. She was hoping that if he said yes, we might then invite him to join us for a nice visit at the café, where she would enjoy hot chocolate. Aimee, always eager for new social encounters, did everything but invite herself.

In Poland, even after a four-year absence, Aimee remembered every therapist by name and was thrilled to see them all again. It amazed me that she remembered the administrative assistant in the office, the maids, even Mr. Franik the custodian. Our new interpreter, Antonella, knew I was Aimee's grandmother and remembered us from previous trips. She was curious about the relationship Aimee and I shared.

As she got to know us, she began to understand my desire to provide every opportunity for Aimee. In the course of our month there, Antonella became a key player in the success of our trip. Born in Italy but an American citizen, Antonella moved to Poland when she married. She and her husband, both trilingual, had served as interpreters at Euromed for a number of years. Passionate about their work and compassionate about the children, their service went far beyond their professional duties.

Antonella developed a deep fondness for Aimee. She told me often that she initially wondered how Aimee would respond to the many demands that would be placed on her in therapy. As the weeks progressed, she was impressed with Aimee's resolve. Aimee likewise loved Antonella and her husband, Bogie. They invited us to their home on several occasions and helped us with errands.

During the second week of our stay, while observing Aimee in spider therapy, I scooted forward on a small footstool in the corner of the gym. As I lifted myself slightly to move forward, I didn't realize my left hand was under the edge of the stool. Down it came on my thumb and I winced in pain and held my hand, trying to be quiet so as not to interrupt Aimee. Within days, my thumb was swollen, throbbing, and painful. A week later, at Antonella's insistence, she accompanied me to the nurse's office where I was immediately referred to a local physician.

Antonella came along to interpret. Dr. Lewinsky, trained in New England, was shy and reserved but confirmed my suspicions that I had a fractured thumb. He concluded that he would have to do surgery to remove the nail but first wanted his diagnosis confirmed with an X-ray. Meanwhile, he wrapped my hand. Bogie drove me to the hospital in Koszalin for X-rays while Antonella remained with Aimee in Mielno. Luckily, Mel was arriving that afternoon.

Fracture confirmed, we made a return trip to the doctor's office. Mel and Aimee joined me there and sat near me in the examining room as Dr. Lewinsky gathered instruments and unwrapped rolls of casting material. Aimee, not seeing well but hearing it all, wanted to know what was happening. She knew what a cast was and continually chattered in the background. "Who is he? What's his name?" she asked. "Grammy, does it hurt? Are you crying? What's he doing now?"

It was fortunate that Mel arrived when he did. He gladly helped with Aimee and performed the tasks I could not. I wore the cast for the remainder of our stay.

• • •

When we returned home, the children were on summer break. We invited each grandchild to spend time with us alone, usually at our small beach house where they enjoyed seaside activities. We invited Aimee often, not only to provide a change of activity for her but also to give Jason and Janise a break in dealing with three children, all with different activities and needs.

One weekend while on the coast, we took a drive to Carmel. It was the first clear day following a week of unusually fierce storms. Aimee enjoyed the laid-back atmosphere as we browsed shops and galleries in the village in the company of our dog, Griffie. In the late afternoon, we enjoyed a scrumptious meal on the patio at a favorite Carmel restaurant.

We returned home that evening and began to unload the car. The boardwalk path to our unit follows ascending curves bordered with natural landscaping of large old Monterey pines and cypress trees. Aimee had been sleeping during the drive home and, rather than placing her in her chair, Mel was carrying her. I took her wheelchair, grabbed the dog's leash, and proceeded up the path.

I suddenly heard a thunderous "crack" and turned in horror as a well-established 40-foot tree came crashing down on the boardwalk, missing Mel and Aimee by inches. It crushed everything in its path, consuming the entire lower section of the walkway and parking lot, narrowly missing our vehicles. We had been blessed. A guardian angel had protected us from catastrophe.

• • •

The twin's birthday, always celebrated in the heat of summer, was open to a variety of considerations and options. As Chloe became more involved with her school friends, she wanted sleepovers and swim parties. Aimee, whose presence, unfortunately, often ruined the fun for Chloe, would stay with us either in Modesto or San Jose. Most of Aimee's friends at school had special needs. At my urging, I encouraged Janise to contact their parents and plan a separate party for Aimee. I agreed to help.

Aimee delivered the invitations to her friends at school and anticipated her party with much excitement. Her best friend, her "boyfriend" as she called him, was Jacob. We all knew Jacob because Aimee talked about him constantly, blushing and giggling as she did so. Jacob is also a child with special needs; however, he is able to walk. He is also one of the few children in Aimee's class who can speak. The mention of Jacob brings a smile to Aimee's face like none other. He adored her as well and openly expressed his genuine affection for Aimee to the teacher, Janise, and even to me when I visited. "I like Aimee so much, Grandma," he said. "Do you think she likes me too?" If only he knew, I thought. She loved him and said it often.

Two weeks before the party, Janise became concerned when no one had responded. We held our breath, hoping that Aimee's first party wouldn't be a failure. It would be so disappointing to her. Finally, two days before the party, Jacob's grandmother, with whom he lived, called to say he had been out of town but was delighted to be invited to Aimee's party. He would be there! Finally the day arrived and Aimee's only guest, other than Chloe, was Jacob. It didn't matter to Aimee; he was all she cared about. They wore their party hats and enjoyed games, finger painting, and eating cake and ice cream together. They laughed and held hands and he helped her open her gifts. He made her a special card, which he read, and a beaded necklace that he proudly placed over her head with gentle care. We were spellbound when, as he was leaning against her chair, they held hands in a show of innocent and heartfelt affection for each other. It meant so much for Aimee to be like Chloe and have friends of her own. It made me very happy that she was able to experience a birthday party the way she wanted it.

Chloe, popular and well liked, had her swim party the following day. She had ten little girls. Aimee knew them all and stayed to eat hotdogs with them, after which we left. I had agreed we would help Jason and Janise by taking Aimee to a movie so she wouldn't feel left out and they could supervise Chloe and her friends.

• • •

Sometimes Aimee asks poignant questions that tug at your heart. One day she asked me, "Grammy, what does it mean to be handicapped?" She caught me completely off guard. I wasn't expecting her to ask that and didn't know how to respond.

"It means that you have special needs that are different from other children," I replied after a pause.

"No, it doesn't!" she said. "It means to be bored in your chair, and it makes me sad." My heart broke for her. It must be terrible to watch the world go by, helpless, as you depend on others for your care and entertainment.

I reassured her that there were many things she *could* do and that she had countless gifts, especially because she could speak, hear, and see. And, she reminded me, "sing and listen to music too."

POLAND ONE LAST TIME

IN SEPTEMBER, it was time for Aimee's annual fund-raiser dinner. The businessmen in Modesto continued to organize the event, which was increasing in support and popularity. It was well attended, and the same guests returned year after year to support the ever-increasing cost of Aimee's therapy. Each year, the regular attendees would marvel at Aimee's growth and progress.

A local columnist heard about Aimee and contacted Janise about doing a short article about her. When he came to their home to meet Aimee and interview Janise, he was so impressed and inspired that he wrote a full-length feature story instead. On Sunday morning, six days before the event, the paper covered Aimee's story on a full front and back page. It was factual and inspiring and touched many hearts.

Aimee loved the attention and recognition. Quite a young lady at nine years old, she sat proudly in her chair, tall and lanky, welcoming guests with her big smile. A large video screen behind her displayed her in action during therapy, in her walker and riding her tricycle. She had accomplished so much.

The disc jockey set up his station, and Aimee insisted that we talk with him. She wanted to know *exactly* what kind of music he intended to play. Dressed in Western wear—red cowboy boots and all—she wanted to hear and dance to Johnny Cash. I knew if I took her out of her chair, I'd never be able to stop. "Dancing" with Aimee is holding her up, under the arms, as you lean forward to grip her and dance as she jumps and kicks her feet to the music. She *expects* that you dance, too, not just stand! This is exhausting and after one, two, or possibly three songs, I am at my limit. I taught Aimee to do the cha-cha-cha, a rhythm she loves and continually wanted to dance to.

"Do you have the cha-cha-cha?" she asked him. When he replied "No," I was relieved!

• • •

Aimee's growth had impaired her progress somewhat. Unfortunately, for most cerebral palsy children, growth only tightens the muscles, making it more difficult to maintain the gains in mobility that they made when smaller and younger. As their bodies grow and approach puberty, they require more strength to support body movement and, although achievable, progress begins to diminish with age.

We were heading back to Poland for another month of therapy in October 2006. Jason and Janise had bought a home on the outskirts of town in a rural area. Aimee, now nine, would be required to change schools, and this concerned me a great deal. She had attended only one school and had been very happy there. And her beloved Jacob would no longer be her classmate. Her new school operated on a different time schedule, perhaps one that would be better for Aimee, all things considered. She would attend school for three months and be off for one. This would reduce the boredom during long summer vacations and would ease the pressure on Janise, who would no longer have to deal with all three kids home for the summer for three months straight.

Before we left for Poland, Aimee said good-bye to her friends at school. They had a farewell day for her. I was busy getting ready for our trip, so I didn't go. In truth, I stayed away because I thought it would be a very sad parting for Aimee. Janise told me that children of all ages and grade levels waited in a line that went around the playground, just to say good-bye. They brought handmade cards, balloons, and gifts for Aimee. She knew Aimee was popular and well liked but had no idea how much Aimee had inspired the other students, until one by one, they expressed their gratitude for her friendship.

• • •

Our flight schedule was straightforward, San Francisco to New York to Berlin. This time, I traveled with Aimee's new stroller instead of her wheelchair. Light and collapsible, it could be carried in the cabin of the plane. Armed with the ADA guidelines for U.S. carriers, I was primed to meet challenges head-on. We were refused stowage of Aimee's stroller when we boarded the plane, and I explained that it was her only mobility and needed to be onboard with us. Although challenged initially, our flight attendants did their best to accommodate us and make us comfortable. For her part, Aimee solicited the friendship of the attendants in our cabin from the moment we set foot on the plane. Perhaps she has learned that this will secure lots of attention and good service on the flight.

We arrived in Berlin rested, greeted by Christian. It was fall now, and the five-hour drive across the Polish countryside was gorgeous. We arrived at Euromed, and within the hour Antonella had arrived with a hugs and kisses and a bag of goodies. I was happy to see her again and knew that if I needed anything, she would be there for me, and that gave me great comfort.

On this visit there was only one other American family at the center. They were from Oregon. The oldest daughter was receiving therapy and could walk independently but still required the occasional use of a wheelchair. She was one year older than Aimee, and her sister a year younger.

Another English-speaking family arrived from London on our second day. Their daughter, a darling blonde girl, was Aimee's age. They sat across the aisle from us in the dining room; it was their first trip. Gillian could stand independently and walk a little and had done very well by the end of the therapy session.

Both of the girls receiving therapy could speak, and this was a plus for Aimee. Many of her peers cannot speak, although they manage to communicate in one way or another. Aimee had the time of her life with her new friends, especially because they included her in everything they did. Because of this, I thought it was one of the most enjoyable sessions Aimee had ever experienced.

The routine was the same, but this time I noticed something different. Aimee had grown up before my eyes. Mature, able to converse, and holding her own in play with the other girls who were far less disabled than she, Aimee joined them as they played school, read books, watched movies, or played Aimee's favorite, Barbie.com, on the computer. They talked before therapy, greeted each other by holding hands in the morning, and sometimes shared the same gym when schedules permitted. Inseparable, they played together every afternoon until dinner was served. Aimee had a ball.

Of course, Chloe and Aimee played together at home. But Chloe has her own friends, busily coming and going, and so Aimee often spends time alone or with her mother. In Poland, Aimee made her own friends. I could see how much that meant to her. They loved Aimee, too, taking her with them as they went off to their secret clubhouse in the corner of the hall. It pleased me to see Aimee develop in this way. Sometimes they would tell Aimee what to do. I observed but didn't interfere and was proud of her when she could hold her own and remain independent.

There were approximately thirty other families at the center from around the globe: Italy, England, Pakistan, India, Germany, and Poland. One of the benefits of a foreign center is that it gave us a chance to make new friends and learn about people from other parts of the world. Nothing did that like a party. Every Saturday night, the center had a "disco" party for the children, complete with mirrored ballroom sphere and refreshments. Aimee couldn't wait and talked about the party all day, anticipating music and dancing.

Initially, when you see these children, from toddlers to late teens, dance together, in or out of their wheelchairs, it is shocking. How can they dance? But they do, and they love it. You soon realize that they are no different from anyone else in their desire to dance and have fun. Aimee, throwing her head back with screams and squeals, "rocking out" to the music, as she would say, would literally not stop until she, or I, dropped. She would boldly ask one of the fathers to dance with her if I could not, or would not, continue. And, of course, no one would refuse her.

Physically, she improved, but her progress was slow. The therapists asked Aimee about her goal and what *she* hoped to achieve by the end of the session. She responded, "My dream is to crawl on the floor! I want to crawl and I want to sit!" she said. No one told her what to say, no one coached her, she simply responded on her own. Unable to sit or stand independently, Aimee still hoped to crawl. The therapists worked with her arms for the entire month, hoping to develop enough strength in them to bear weight in a crawling position. She was almost there, they said, and suggested we stay another month, but we could not.

One day when we finished her therapy she said, "Thank you, Grammy for taking me for exercises." I asked her if she liked it and she said, "No, but it makes me strong. It hurts but it makes me strong!" I've always believed that she understands what I do and that I do it to empower her to feel better about herself.

One morning, I turned on the only English television station to listen to the news.

They were broadcasting information about the war. Aimee began asking, "Who died? How many died? Why did they die? Where are they?" She asked the questions so fast I hardly had time to answer before she asked the next. I didn't know how to explain in terms she would understand but said they were talking about the "war."

"What's war?" she asked. I explained that it was when countries send soldiers to fight for their country. "Oh, I get it," she said. "I fight with Chloe, too!"

"You do?" I inquired, "Why?"

"Because she takes my CD player and my iPod away, that's why!" she exclaimed.

• • •

We were in Poland for Halloween and I had packed a costume for Aimee. She was a "disco queen." She wore the costume the entire day, complete with makeup and purple hair! They do not celebrate Halloween in Poland, so Mel had shipped a box of Halloween treats prior to our arrival. We had plenty of treats and favors for all the children so that they could experience Halloween with us. Some parents decorated the halls with ribbons, lights, and party favors, and we hosted a party for the kids. Everyone came in costumes or makeup—there were gypsies, doctors, brides, ghosts, witches, and a variety of creative characters. It was great fun!

Mel arrived and surprised Aimee when he did so. He spent the last week with us in Poland and planned a few days for us to sightsee in and around Berlin. He enjoyed taking Aimee to therapy, and I relaxed a little and enjoyed visiting with Antonella over a cup of coffee every morning. In the evenings, we socialized with other parents while the girls played. One evening, concluding their play, Aimee said, "Grammy, we just had our secret girl's *Rotary* meeting." Mel and I are deeply involved with Rotary International and it delighted me that Aimee thought of herself as one of us.

The therapy was coming to a close. Socially, she had made great strides and was the girl everyone wanted to be around. Aimee's physical gains were minimal compared to other sessions. Our goal now is to maintain the status quo so she doesn't lose the ground she's gained physically. She may never walk or crawl, but she deserves the opportunity to be the best she can be. I don't know what the future will bring for her, but I intend to be there, no matter what.

BLESSINGS

CHAPTER 21

AIMEE WILL BE TEN YEARS OLD this year. I reflect now on these years, years that I could have never imagined. Ten years ago, I had it all—I knew exactly who and what I was. But time would prove me wrong. I did not know Aimee. Through her I discovered the depth of my own character, the power of my love, the conviction of my faith, and my courage in the face of hopelessness and despair.

As a grandparent I could have walked away, saying that this sad situation was not my responsibility. Instead, I decided to get involved and live the example of commitment to family that I had learned from my own parents. It was a question of responsibility and what I wished to do about it. I didn't think about it then or ruminate over what I should or should not do. It simply flowed like life does when it takes you down a river, twisting, turning, and sometimes raging out of control. I followed my heart and my conscience, which took me on a difficult journey that has enriched my life.

The love I felt for Aimee in the beginning caught me by surprise. For me, enraptured the first time I held her, captivated by her determination to live, there was no choice. The love that Aimee and I share brought out our determination and resolve, giving each of us strength to move forward. I felt the full potency of life in the power of that love. It is what has made Aimee who she is. She wasn't abandoned or forgotten, but instead, was treasured and embraced—as all life should be.

• • •

The last ten years also have taught me about the power of prayer and the influence of a higher authority in our lives. Hundreds, if not thousands, of prayers have been said for Aimee and, I suppose, for me, too. I had faith that we would not be left adrift and that Aimee would be given something of value, one "gift" that would help her live to her fullest potential. My prayers were answered when she began to speak. But Aimee's message is not only verbal but also spiritual. She sets an example of hope that rings eternal. There are always new discoveries, new opportunities, and new challenges in achieving life's dreams.

Nothing worth doing comes easily, and certainly not without preparation and commitment to reaching beyond yourself. These have always been values that describe me. During these years with Aimee, my character traits were challenged beyond comprehension. I never imagined in the beginning that I had what it takes to do what I have done. I would not have imagined that my own commitment and stubborn drive, even at the risk of my own life, would help give Aimee the chance to achieve.

As a Girl Scout in my youth, I've lived by and have never forgotten my pledge to "do my best" and "be prepared." My determination to educate myself about cerebral palsy and all aspects of Aimee's care gave me the confidence to move forward with my convictions. What if we had accepted the prognosis for her at birth? What if we didn't love, didn't have faith, or didn't believe that every life has value?

A dictionary will tell you that the definition of courage is "the ability to face danger, difficulty, or uncertainty without being overcome by fear." In the beginning, I was overcome by a dreadful fear that consumed me. Then, I changed my life. I made a sacrifice—for the good of another human being. This led me down an arduous, but rewarding, path—one that I will continue to follow.

I'm not a patient person. I make decisions quickly and stand by them. But it took patience to relinquish control to others when the decision was not mine. I learned that patience allowed others to find their own way and put their trust in me. I taught Aimee the value and meaning of trust. I wholeheartedly believe that Aimee and I have earned the respect of those around us through our example of love, courage, patience, and trust.

I am at peace with myself now. The journey has not always gone as I had hoped, but I am grateful for so many things that have gone better than expected. I have achieved my dream of telling Aimee's story to inspire others not to be afraid to follow their hearts. And, in doing so, I hope to have become a serious advocate for all children with special needs.

What about Aimee? I can finally let go of the worry and fear of what might happen to her. She has a happy and fulfilling life. Not a perfect life, but life nonetheless. She may never experience the joy of walking independently, running, or jumping rope with her friends—but she will continue to experience the joy of immense love that surrounds her. She is content. I can say the same for me.

We have been rewarded with the precious gift of her life and would not change her for anything in the world. It has been the gift of a lifetime and a journey I would not have taken alone. I did it for the love of one little girl. I did it for the love of Aimee.

EPILOGUE

EVERYONE HAS A STORY but not everyone is an open book. Although
our story has already been shared with you, what appears to be the end
is only a continuation of what has happened and what is to come. No
matter how secure and comfortable our daily lives seem to be as they
unfold, nothing remains the same.

That is how it is with Aimee and me. I still cannot avoid asking
myself on occasion the *what if* question. *What if* Aimee had been
born normal? *What if* Aimee were able to walk? *What if* Aimee could
see, read, and write? *What if* she had a normal twin-sister relationship? Although I know these are pointless questions, and ones I should
not ask, I cannot help but consider the possibilities of a different direction in life for Aimee.

• • •

One bright spring day while driving back to San Jose with Aimee so
that she could spend the weekend, she said she wanted to tell me something. "Okay" I said, "What do you want to tell me?" She replied, "My
mommy is moving out; she wants to be *separated*."

"What!" Stunned, I could hardly believe what I had heard and asked her to repeat it again just in case I didn't hear it right. She repeated it and this time insisted it was true. Knowing Aimee, I understood that she wanted to relieve herself of this "secret" burden and wanted to talk about it. I also had the sense that she wanted to sensationalize the situation and add some shock value in telling me. Indeed, I was stunned but not entirely surprised. I had no doubt Aimee was telling the truth in her own innocent way.

I had sensed some tension between Jason and Janise in recent months but barely enough to raise my intuitive awareness of the situation. Now, I didn't want to pry, but I couldn't stop myself from asking Aimee a few questions.

"How do you know that, Aimee?" I asked. "Because my mommy and daddy fight and they are not going to live together anymore!" she replied. When I asked her how she felt about it, she said she was "very sad" and "didn't like it." But, she insisted, "I'm okay, Grammy." My immediate response was to play it down, but inside, I was extremely concerned and sad. I worried what would happen to the children. In particular, I wondered how they would manage Aimee's care and how she would cope with the changes that would undoubtedly be forced on her.

When we returned home, I told Mel and he, too, shared my concerns. We decided to be supportive of Aimee and talk about it with her only if she initiated the conversation. Otherwise, we would wait until her parents announced the circumstances of this devastating situation. That happened soon enough and things quickly got worse. But that's another story, their story, so I will only focus on the effect it had on Aimee.

At first Aimee seemed to do well. Even her teacher was surprised and impressed with her resilience during such a difficult time. She seemingly adjusted to the changes: the moves to two new and different households, new schools, and new schedules. She no longer would have her own bedroom but would have to combine her things with her siblings in order to accommodate the new living arrangements. And, she would have to share a bed with someone else.

Unlike most kids, Aimee has few objects she can call her very own. Her books, CDs, an iPod, and a small number of toys and trinkets mean everything to her. Because of her sight and physical limitations, she cannot command control of many toys. Still, at our home and when we travel for extensive periods of time, I always give her a space for her special things. She knows exactly what she has and instructs me where to find and return each item to "her shelf." This might sound simple, but to her it means control of a small space that she can claim as her very own. When everyone moved and her belongings were scattered and combined with those of her siblings, she told me she had "lost her things." I encouraged Jason to create a small bookshelf where Aimee could have her own collection of prized items in a secure and safe place. To his credit, Jason acknowledged the importance of a space for her and did just that.

In time, one way or another, things seem to work out. Jason, suddenly overwhelmed with the duties of a single parent and without another adult in the household to share the load, was forced to become more involved with Aimee's day-to-day care. One morning when I arrived at his home at 7:00 a.m. to pick up Aimee for a doctor's appointment in Sacramento, he had already fed her breakfast, dressed her in a well-coordinated outfit and brushed her teeth, and he was combing her hair into a ponytail. I was impressed. This wasn't easy for Jason, but he managed to cope, handle his responsibilities, and move on. There had been, and would continue to be, many hard times ahead.

• • •

Aimee survived these changes, but not without some difficulty. She experienced some problems, which manifested themselves in her not eating, using naughty language, and sometimes acting defiantly. In spite of it all, she continued to do well, overcome the changes in her life, and advance to the best of her ability.

Years of therapy have satisfactorily maintained Aimee's physical condition by keeping her body aligned and as strong as possible. But, as she gets older, bigger, and even taller, the challenge to maintain that status becomes more and more difficult. There is not much more we can do—medication, therapy, and Botox injections are the treatments of choice. We have now added a regime of Botox injections to Aimee's treatment, which requires me to make the trip from San Jose to Modesto to Sacramento every six weeks. The effects of the Botox last approximately three months, during which time Aimee is able to move her body in a more controlled and relaxed manner. This enables her to do tasks that she normally cannot do, such as feeding herself, coloring, and using the computer. This repetitive ability to use her arms and legs helps develop muscles that are otherwise not used because of the CP.

Her injections are scheduled in the outpatient surgical unit and require that Aimee be anaesthetized for the delicate procedure. The all-day, and sometimes overnight, trip means nothing to eat prior to the injections and the usual post-op nausea afterward. Even so, Aimee handles it all with a smile while keeping the hospital staff impressed with her courage and entertained with her humor. I try my best to make it as pleasant an experience for Aimee as possible, but I still remain anxious about the reality of the risks involved.

Aimee wants to be in control and more independent than ever, doing everything by herself even though this is not totally possible. She recognizes that kids around her are able to do things for themselves, and she wants to be like them. To support and encourage her in this goal as she grows and matures, I continue to take her for month-long therapy sessions twice a year. We have not returned to Poland recently, although it remains a viable possibility in the future. We have opted for the convenience of travel to Southern California for the therapy instead.

Consistent with girls her age, Aimee has matured into a young lady who enjoys shopping for clothes, shoes, and accessories. She even likes her nails polished and, once in a while, lip gloss and a little blusher on her cheeks. Long baths, lotion, perfume, and a special hairstyle finish the "spa" treatment when she visits.

She loves music still and can identify every artist and song on the current top-twenty lists and beyond. Because she cannot read or write, she memorizes everything she needs to know and recalls that information when it suits her and can spell simple words from memory. She even makes up jokes, stories, and poems.

Recently, while eating in a French restaurant with Mel and me during a therapy stint in Southern California, a boy and his parents were seated at a table near us. Aimee thought the boy looked like a boy she had met at the hotel a few days earlier. His name was Sam. While thinking about "Sam" she began reciting the lines from *Green Eggs and Ham*. As she did so, she continued substituting her own words to the verse:

I like this restaurant, yes I do!
I like to come, and eat here too!
I do, I like it, with my friend Sam,
I like to eat here because I can!

I couldn't write it fast enough to get it all, but I was extremely impressed. Although simple and not perfect, I thought her ability was remarkable for a girl who cannot read or write.

• • •

Aimee's siblings have enriched her life as much as she has enriched theirs. Identical twins share a special bond, and Aimee adores being with Chloe. Time together provides her with a best-friend relationship she might not otherwise experience. Music and current trends provide the girls with plenty to do. To Aimee's delight, Chloe selects her outfits for school, combs her hair, and keeps her nails polished in a variety of metallic colors.

Chloe is an award-winning athlete, competitive and tough. I often wonder what Aimee thinks when she watches her sister play soccer. As much as I know Aimee would love to run, I believe she is inspired by her sister's accomplishments which, in turn, encourage her to meet her own goals. Chloe, easygoing and loving, is always there to support her.

Jeffrey, as a boy, relates to Aimee in a slightly different way. Emotional, compassionate, and kind, he is always willing to lend a helping hand and assist in whatever requests are made of him. He often reads to her and enjoys the undivided attention when telling her one of his original stories. As he matures, he has a better understanding of the demands of Aimee's care and her needs and, rather than compete, he takes her needs in stride.

One day, while traveling alone in the car with Chloe and Jeffrey, they surprised me by asking if they could ask some questions about Aimee. I encouraged them to do so and was touched by their curiosity about what would happen to Aimee and them as they got older. I explained the best I could that she would never walk and would always require care.

Although their sadness was palpable, it was a great opportunity to praise them for their loving support and kindness toward Aimee. After all, it cannot be easy for children to continually exhibit tolerance and patience while they wait to have their own needs met. Yet, to their credit, I've never heard either of them complain. I'm especially proud of them for their outstanding example of compassion as advocates of children with special needs.

• • •

Aimee has a mind of her own, with definite likes and dislikes, and she doesn't hesitate to make her sentiments known to others. She wants to make her own decisions about what she eats, wears, and does. As with all children her age, acceptance is important. I respect her wishes and encourage her to speak up for herself and to openly express her wants and needs to those around her. She is a winner in my book, and I tell her that "winners" always describe what they want and need. She understands that she alone must communicate her desires to others.

This is especially true at school, where she interacts with teachers, aides, and peers. School provides her with academic challenges and happy social interaction. She is conscientious about how she looks to others, especially males. One special male in Aimee's life has been her loyal and loving "boyfriend," Jacob. When she changed schools, everyone expressed concern over how she would deal with separation from her friend. As it turned out, she missed him terribly, but when she returned to her former school, they were reunited to their mutual joy and delight. Then, he went off to junior high, and again, separation. Fortunately for them both, they are once again sharing a classroom. We all know and love Jacob, and Aimee delights in talking about him constantly! He is, undoubtedly, her best friend and, because he is not in a wheelchair, can push her around in her chair and entertain her with his antics. Her relationship with Jacob is a loving and important one and, although innocent in nature, demonstrates how valuable mutually reciprocated emotions and affection are to us all. Aimee often tells me to make her look cute or pretty when going out because she doesn't want to have "stinky breath," "dirty hair," or, the worse offense possible, "body odor"!

Aimee understands that how she relates to others determines how they are influenced and respond to her in return. She exudes confidence in her social skills; however, her obvious physical disability often unjustly defines who she is. First impressions count, especially for kids. They often cannot look beyond her disabilities to see the person inside and instead avoid approaching her chair, even at her invitation to do so. A person's disability should not define that person's life or character, but unfortunately, even today, it does. Sadly, I've observed this many times and it often brings me to the brink of tears.

Children can be cruel and often rude to a child who is not able to approach others on her own and must be approached by others first. Aimee is reliant on someone else to push her chair forward to meet another individual, and this usually doesn't happen. Even though she joyfully invites new kids to come forward and talk with her, engaging them with questions and funny comments, they remain hesitant. Some are responsive and talk with her, while others whisper, frown, and back away without a word. Even after all these years, I still feel disheartened when this happens because it seems so unfair.

• • •

Aimee now attends junior high school and, for the first time in their lives, she and Chloe attend the same school. Chloe has embraced this idea and has expressed her enthusiasm as a volunteer helper in Aimee's classroom. Aimee considers Chloe's vast circle of friends to be her own as well. Junior high has brought Aimee new and exciting challenges and goals. She continues to use an adaptive computer in the classroom and now changes classes throughout the day. Children with special needs are transitioned into the appropriate class curriculum while accommodating their individual needs and interests. Aimee's plans include learning a percussion instrument. Band is her scheduled elective; she will use a special adaptive drum that fastens to her wheelchair. I can hardly wait to hear her perform—and have no doubt she will keep her fellow band members entertained.

For the first time, physical education and exercise are incorporated into her curriculum, and she now walks the halls in her gait trainer with the help of her aide for twenty minutes each day. This delights Aimee because she can engage the attention of fellow students to watch her "walk."

Without the love of family and relatives, including grandparents, aunts, uncles, and cousins; the support of teachers and aides; the friendship of classmates; and the help of so many individuals along the way, Aimee would not have the self-confidence or quality of life she enjoys today. The depth of her character and personality are so much more than meets the eye. Filled as she is with love for others, the concept of appreciation and gratefulness for her blessings is not beyond her understanding. Quite the contrary, she appreciates all the support and love that she has been showered with over the years. We all give back in whatever way we can, and I have encouraged Aimee to do the same in her own way. There is something we can each do, or give, to benefit another. For Aimee, it turns out to be her hair.

One day while she was watching a morning show on TV, a segment was presented on donating hair. Aimee was intrigued and listened intently as they talked about children with cancer and other diseases that resulted in total hair loss. A group of teen girls were cutting their hair on TV and donating it to Locks of Love, an organization that processes the donated hair into wigs for children. I explained to Aimee how the process worked, and she said, "Grammy, I want to give my hair to a little girl who has no hair." Her announcement flabbergasted me. I explained that it would require growing her hair very long and that she would have to tolerate its being brushed and combed, which might be more difficult for her than her current short, and easy-to-manage, "bob" hairstyle. She insisted that she wanted to do it, and I agreed that it was a marvelous and wonderful thing she could do to help another child in need. Aimee and I explained it all to her parents, and they agreed to help her meet her goal.

It took over two years for Aimee to grow and donate her hair. It was not always easy for her to tolerate the brushing and braiding, but she did it. She mentioned it every day and told everyone who commented on her hair why she was letting it grow. I'm so proud of her for making this commitment by herself and sticking to it. More important, I'm proud of her for wanting to give so generously of the one thing she has to donate—her beautiful long hair.

Finally, on a cool October day, I took her to the salon where, for the first time, she managed to sit independently in the chair and watch in the mirror as her long braids were cut and wrapped for mailing to Locks of Love. She was thrilled with her accomplishment and delighted that her hair was going to be made into a wig for "a little girl with no hair." Looking adorable in her new short hairdo, she quickly expressed her desire to grow her hair again and "give it to another little girl." Her sincere expression of joy in giving something of herself made me love her even more.

In spite of all her physical challenges, and the emotional ones in the recent past, Aimee continues to smile her engaging smile and find joy and happiness in each day. Her fortitude to survive often complex and chaotic changes beyond her control speaks of her immense will and determination to overcome and do her best. She continues to understand more about herself and what she is capable of achieving through dedication and commitment.

Her warm disposition and affectionate smile continue to charm all who meet her. There is something magical in her presence, and her sense of humor keeps everyone entertained and laughing. She is very interested in what happens around her and can even carry on a discussion about current events. Her love of food is secondary only to her passion for music, and her keen sense of smell and taste have contributed to her interest in watching the Food Network as the cooks discuss the many ingredients in the cooking process. She enjoys the kitchen and savors the smell and taste of food as it is being prepared. Eating out gives Aimee the opportunity to taste and critique different cuisines of the world—all of which she enjoys with gusto.

. . .

It's been a wonderful journey. Aimee is almost a teenager and I am almost a senior. Neither of us knows where our path will lead us in the future, but we know that we will continue on it together as long as we can, to do whatever it takes to make the quality of Aimee's life, and the lives of children like her, the best it can be. I cannot imagine life without Aimee or the deep bond and love we have shared. Instead of asking myself the old *what if* question of what could have been, I ask myself instead, *what if* she had never been born.

Without Aimee just the way she is, I would have missed out on the experience of a lifetime. I would have missed the self-satisfaction of overcoming personal challenges. I would, most likely, have never known my own capacity for devotion to a grandchild in need who was wanting to be loved and acknowledged as a valued human being. I would never have understood what it means to truly respect another individual, body and soul, for who rather than what they are. Most of all, I would not have known that faith and hope are at the heart of our existence, no matter what kind of existence it is.

Without Aimee this story would not have been told. I would never have dreamed of writing it, nor would I have experienced the heartfelt joy I've felt in sharing it with you. I hope you have enjoyed our journey. The opportunity is there for everyone, especially parents and grandparents, to make a difference. All you need to do is extend your hand and open your heart to a child in need to take that first step together on a journey of your own.

AIMEE'S PHOTO ALBUM

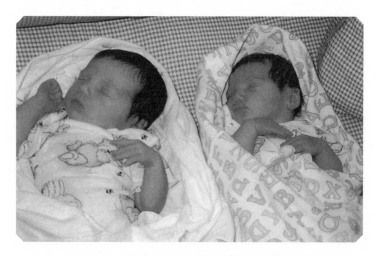

Newborn twins, August 1997

Janise and Jason holding Aimee and Chloe at baptism ceremony, 1997

Chloe and Aimee at age 6 months

Julie with Aimee at 1 year

Aimee, age 4, independently standing for the first time
during second therapy trip to Poland, 2001

Mel with Aimee, age 4, enjoying time together

Aimee in her princess costume, age 5, Halloween, 2002

Julie and the twins, age 5, Christmas, 2002

Julie and Aimee on the beach promenade, Mielno, Poland, 2006

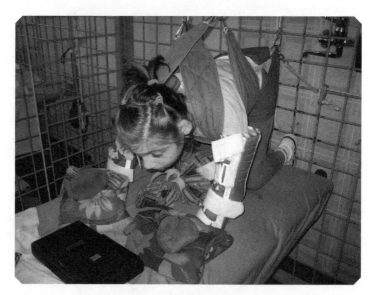

Aimee listening to music while being "positioned" during therapy in Poland

Aimee, age 8, happy and smiling during therapy in Poland

Aimee, age 9, making her First Communion, May 2006

Chloe and Aimee, age 10, in Hawaii with Julie and Mel

Jason with the kids on Father's Day, 2008

Julie with Aimee trying out a new adaptive swing, 2008

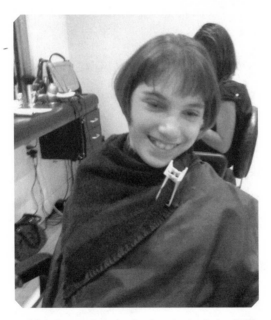

Aimee, age 12, in her new haircut after donating her hair to Locks of Love

About the Author

Julie Riera Matsushima's life took a dramatic turn with the birth of twin granddaughters in 1997. Since accompanying her three-year-old handicapped granddaughter to Poland for cutting-edge cerebral palsy therapy, Julie has tirelessly advocated for children with special needs. In 2001 she established the nonprofit That's Amore Charitable Foundation Inc. to serve children with disabilities. Owner of an interior design and consulting business and a community leader, she serves as a parks commissioner for the City of San Jose Parks, Recreation, and Neighborhood Services Department, where she has raised awareness for the need of adaptive and equal park play equipment. She is also on the advisory board of the Office of Therapeutic Services for the City of San Jose, which serves the needs of disabled citizens in the community.

Julie is the recipient of the prestigious Santa Clara Council of Boy Scouts of America 2008 Character Award and the Santa Clara County

Medici Medallion Award for her work to make public parks and playgrounds accessible to children with special needs. *Metro Silicon Valley* newspaper recognized her in their annual "Profiles in Change," highlighting citizens making a difference, and she has been featured in the *San Jose Business Journal*, *The Rosegarden*, and *Willow Glen Resident*, and *Image Magazine*, among other local publications.

Julie lives in the heart of Silicon Valley with her husband, Mel, and their beloved dog, Griffith. She travels the 150-mile round trip to Modesto, California, regularly to visit with her grandchildren and participate in their activities. She is currently doing research for her second book.